ROUTLEDGE LIBRARY EDITIONS:
POLITICAL THOUGHT AND
POLITICAL PHILOSOPHY

I0028195

Volume 7

THE CONSENT THEORY OF POLITICAL OBLIGATION

THE CONSENT THEORY OF POLITICAL OBLIGATION

HARRY BERAN

Routledge
Taylor & Francis Group

LONDON AND NEW YORK

First published in 1987 by Croom Helm Ltd

This edition first published in 2020
by Routledge
2 Park Square, Milton Park, Abingdon, Oxon OX14 4RN

and by Routledge
52 Vanderbilt Avenue, New York, NY 10017

Routledge is an imprint of the Taylor & Francis Group, an informa business

British Library Cataloguing in Publication Data
A catalogue record for this book is available from the British Library

ISBN: 978-0-367-21961-1 (Set)
ISBN: 978-0-429-35434-2 (Set) (ebk)
ISBN: 978-0-367-23084-5 (Volume 7) (hbk)
ISBN: 978-0-367-23089-0 (Volume 7) (pbk)
ISBN: 978-0-429-27828-0 (Volume 7) (ebk)

Publisher's Note
The publisher has gone to great lengths to ensure the quality of this reprint but points out that some imperfections in the original copies may be apparent.

Disclaimer
The publisher has made every effort to trace copyright holders and would welcome correspondence from those they have been unable to trace.

The Consent Theory of Political Obligation

Harry Beran

CROOM HELM
London • New York • Sydney

© 1987 Harry Beran
Croom Helm Publishers Ltd, Provident House,
Burrell Row, Beckenham, Kent BR3 1AT
Croom Helm Australia, 44–50 Waterloo Road,
North Ryde, 2113, New South Wales

British Library Cataloguing in Publication Data
Beran, Harry
    The consent theory of political obligation.
    — (Croom Helm international series in
    social and political thought)
    1. Allegiance
    I. Title
    323.6'.5   JC328
    ISBN 0-7099-5077-2

Published in the USA by
Croom Helm
in association with Methuen, Inc.
29 West 35th Street
New York, NY 10001

Library of Congress Cataloging-in-Publication Data
Beran, Harry.
    The consent theory of political obligation.

    (Croom Helm international series in social and
political thought)
    Bibliography: p.
    Includes index.
    1. Consensus (Social sciences) 2. Legitimacy of
governments. 3. Liberty. I. Title. II. Series.
JC328.2.B46 1987   320.01'1   87-13574
ISBN 0-7099-5077-2

Printed and bound in Great Britain
by Billing & Sons Limited, Worcester.

Contents

Contents

Acknowledgements

This version of consent theory began its life as a doctoral dissertation in 1973 and has constantly evolved since then. Many colleagues have provided encouragement, suggestions and helpful criticism of various kinds, among them Preston King, John McCloskey, John Charvet, John Kilkullen, Regina Pacher-Theinburg, George Molnar, the late Stanley Benn, the late John Plamenatz, Carole Pateman, Keith Campbell, Paul Brownsey, Michael Lesnoff, David Lloyd-Thomas and Michael Jackson. It only remains to extend my thanks for such help and to express my regret for any failure to make better use of it.

I would also like to thank Bill Ireson for his helpful suggestions and for preparing the manuscript for press; and Joan Hutchinson and Dianne Smith-Cullen who produced the original typescript with amazing grace, speed and competence.

In Chapters 2, 3, 5 and 6, I use ideas previously presented in the following articles:

'Ought, Obligation and Duty', *Australasian Journal of Philosophy*, 50 (1972)

'Political Obligation and Democracy', *Australasian Journal of Philosophy*, 54 (1976)

'In Defense of the Consent Theory of Political Obligation and Authority', *Ethics*, 87 (1977)

'What is the Basis of Political Authority?', *The Monist*, 66 (1983)

'A Liberal Theory of Secession', *Political Studies*, XXXII (1984)

My greatest debt is of course to the classics of consent and contract theory.

(In some places the use of personal pronouns can be avoided only by such cumbersome locutions as 'one' or 'he or she'. Until someone invents euphonious sexually neutral pronouns for English, the least evil may be for male authors to use 'he' and female ones to use 'she' in such places.)

Für meine Mutter,
Lisl Arztmiller

1

Introduction

In this book I try to make plausible the claim that, within liberal democratic theory, political obligation and authority must rest on the actual personal consent of citizens.

The book tries to fill a surprising gap in contemporary political theory. The consent theory of political obligation is the most commonly accepted theory of political obligation in the history of Western political philosophy (often of course in the form of contract theory).[1] Even some of its critics grant that it 'has provided us with a more intuitively appealing account of political obligation than any other tradition in modern political theory' (Simmons, 1979, p. 57). In the last two centuries liberal democracies have emerged and with them the widespread belief that political authority rests on the consent of the governed. The American Declaration of Independence provides an early and famous expression of this view in asserting that governments derive 'their just powers from the consent of the governed'. The American Constitution does not repeat this phrase, but students of it claim that its Preamble 'embodies' the principle that the people are sovereign, that any and all authority for governmental action must flow from them and that government at any level may be conducted only with the consent of the governed.[2] Some more recent liberal democratic constitutions express the essence of these ideas explicitly. Thus the 1949 Constitution of the Federal Republic of Germany asserts that 'all state authority emanates from the people' and the 1974 Swedish Constitution begins with the words 'All public power in Sweden emanates from the people'. Yet despite all this, there does not exist a single contemporary attempt to state fully and systematically what the consent is which is supposed to be the basis of political obligation and authority, what place such consent has in a liberal democratic state,

1

and to defend consent theory against the numerous objections to it which occupy a good deal of space in contemporary discussions of political obligation and authority. Moreover, perhaps partly because of the absence of such work, few contemporary political theorists accept consent theory.[3]

Much about restating consent theory in contemporary terms can be learnt from the writers who have, in recent years, written in support of the claim that actual consent is the basis of political obligation and authority. H.D. Lewis (1940) draws attention to the narrow scope of consent theory (he points out that consent is intended to explain only one of the possible moral reasons for obeying the law) and demolishes some of Hume's objections to it. But he does nothing to indicate what consent consists in. Others offer three different accounts as to what it consists in. Joseph Tussman (1960) identifies it with acceptance of membership in the state, but acknowledges that many adult citizens do not accept such membership with the knowledge that this counts as consent. John Plamenatz (1967) and D.D. Raphael (1970) identify it with participation in democratic elections. And H.L.A. Hart (1955, pp. 185-6) and John Rawls (in an early article: 1964) identify it with the acceptance of the benefits of the law-abidingness of one's fellow citizens. Michael Walzer (1970) gives all three forms of consent some role in his account of the extent to which consent can be found in liberal democracies, but considers political participation to be the best expression of it.

All these writers claim or assume that consent-based political obligation and authority is at least possible and actually exists to some substantial extent, in contemporary liberal democracies with their representative form of government. Carole Pateman (1979), however, asserts that the problem of political obligation cannot be solved within liberal democratic theory, partly because it is, she claims, necessarily a theory of representative democracy. She holds that the problem of political obligation can be solved only within a theory of participatory democracy. Pateman appears to identify the consent which creates political obligation with participation in the law-making of direct democracy.

Though all the writers mentioned explicitly support some version of consent theory, none gives anything remotely like a full and systematic exposition or defence of it. To fill this gap I spell out the assumptions of democratic liberalism which, *pace* the utilitarians and *pace* Rawls's cavalier dismissal of actual consent (in *A Theory of Justice* 1971), make it necessary for consistent liberal democratic theory to insist that actual personal consent must be the basis of political obligation and authority. I give a systematic exposition of the theory which, I hope, does justice to the insights of other consent theorists and those of other writers on political obligation and authority; and I provide a case for and full defence of the version of the theory advanced here.

To achieve the greatest possible plausibility for the theory, I:

(a) identify the consent which creates political obligation and authority with acceptance of membership in the state but also give participation in democratic elections and acceptance of the benefits of the law-abidingness of one's fellow citizens important supplementary roles in a theory of justified political obedience;

(b) stress that consent provides only one of the possible reasons for obeying the state, namely that reason which is involved in the existence of an authority relationship between the state and its citizens;

(c) stress that the utility of and consent to the state are, therefore not mutually exclusive, but complementary and equally necessary parts of a liberal democratic theory of justified political obedience;

(d) stress that consent theory need not assume that existing liberal democracies stand in an authority relationship to most of their citizens and is, therefore, not committed to the task of finding acts of actual consent among the present citizens of existing liberal democracies.

Once these features of consent theory are appreciated, some of the often repeated objections to it lose their plausibility. Those which are not diffused by them can also be rebutted.

I develop the version of consent theory I find most plausible in Chapters 3, 4 and 5, qualify it in subsequent chapters and summarise it in Chapter 9. (Readers who like to know the general outline of a theory before its finer points may find it useful to read the summary in Chapter 9 first.)

Notes

1. See Gough (1967). Pitkin introduces her discussion of political obligation and consent with the remark that the doctrine of consent is the solution most commonly offered of the problem of political obligation (1965, p. 990). Compare Pateman (1979, pp. 1–2) and Steinberg, (1978, p. 4).

2. See Hancock (1963, p. 78).

3. Or rather, while there is a great deal of casual appeal to and acceptance of consent as the basis of political obligation (see, e.g. Hoffman, 1981,

and Wight, 1972), most of the writers who particularly focus on and critically discuss political obligation reject consent theory. This is reflected in the present work in the small number of writers who can be mentioned as accepting the theory (see Chapter 1) and the many writers who are mentioned as rejecting it (see Chapters 4 and 6).

2

Conceptual Preliminaries and Normative Assumptions

I am trying to make plausible the thesis that, within liberal democratic theory, the actual personal consent of citizens must be the basis of political authority and political obligation. Since there is much disagreement on the correct analysis of the concepts of *consent, authority* and *obligation*, I will make such analytical remarks about them as I expect to be sufficient to make my use of them clear and plausible. In the last part of the chapter I will note some normative assumptions which I make.

Consent

I will make clear my use of the concept of consent not by analysing it but by using the model of promise. Consenting, agreeing and promising to do X are alike in that they put the person who consents, agrees or promises to do X under an obligation to do X and give the person who receives the consent, agreement or promise a right to X being done. The obligation and the right are correlatives. Both are created by the one act of promising etc. and they are two aspects of the relationship created by the promise between the promiser and the promisee. The obligation and the right are moral ones, since one is morally blameworthy if one fails to do what one has promised or consented or agreed to do, without sufficient moral reasons.

Thus by promising to do X one can create a moral reason for doing X where without the promise, other things being equal, there would be none (e.g. by promising to lend Jane a book) or create an additional moral reason for doing X where there already is a moral reason for doing it independently of the promise (e.g. by promising my mother on her death bed that I will support my aged father).

There are some moral reasons for action which hold independently of one's past acts. In contrast, promising is a device which enables persons to place themselves under a moral obligation by their free choice. Therefore, if one is, for example, coerced to say 'I promise to give you 5,000 dollars' the utterance does not count as a promise and no obligation is created. (The last sentence involves two claims: the conceptual claim that the coerced utterance of the promising formula is not a promise, and the normative — and conceptual — claim that it does not create an obligation. I make both claims on the basis of the assumption that no adequate analysis of the concept of a *promise* can be given without the definition including 'creates a moral obligation'. Hence, if no obligation has been created, no promise has been made. Following J.L. Austin (1965), I say that an attempt to promise which succeeds in creating an obligation 'comes off'.)

Coercion is one way in which a putative promise can fail to come off. There are, of course, other ways . An attempt to promise comes off only if the attempted act is free, informed and competent. Hart has made extremely plausible the view that the best, and perhaps the only adequate, way of specifying whether a putative promise satisfies these three conditions is via a list of further conditions all of which must be *absent* for the attempted promise to come off (1963). Following Hart, I call these further conditions defeating conditions, since, if one has uttered 'I promise to do X' seriously (i.e. not in a joke or play or language lesson etc.), one can still defeat the claim that one has promised to do X, if one can show that one or more of these conditions obtained. The most important of these defeating conditions are the following:[1]

(1) Lack of freedom defence:
(a) coercion;
(b) undue influence;
(c) post-hypnotic suggestion;
(d) exploitation of promiser's predicament.[2]

(2) Inadequate information defence:
(a) deception;
(b) innocent misrepresentation by the promiser of an important matter relevant to the promise;
(c) gross misunderstanding by the promiser and the promisee about a matter relevant to the promise.[3]

(3) Lack of competence defence:
(a) insanity of the promiser (or the promisee for that matter);

(b) temporary or permanent mental incapacity of the promiser (e.g. complete intoxication or senility);
(c) immaturity of the promiser.

There is one possible defeating condition not included in the above list. Some writers claim that a putative promise to do something morally wrong does not create a promissory obligation (and therefore, in my terms, does not come off). I do not include this condition because other writers claim that such a promise does come off and does create a promissory obligation (though one which may be overridden by the wrongness of the promised action) and because I know no entirely persuasive argument for one of the claims rather than the other. At any rate, it is not likely to make any substantive difference to consent theory which of the two positions is adopted. If the immorality of a promised act is a defeating condition, then the general agreement to obey the law fails to come off with respect to the specific law which is morally wrong. If such immorality is not a defeating condition, then the general agreement to obey the law comes off even with respect to the immoral law, but the resulting obligation to obey the immoral law may be overridden by the moral wrongness of the action it requires. I will adopt the latter position for the following reason (which, I grant, does not compel adopting the position). The kind of liberal democratic state which has (consent-based) political authority over the great majority of its citizens can be assumed to be morally desirable on the whole. Still, experience indicates that such a state will at best be only nearly just, i.e. will have some laws which are morally wrong. In agreeing to obey such a state one agrees to do something which is not morally wrong. It, therefore, seems simplest to say that such a promise comes off, *simpliciter*, and creates an obligation to obey all law, even laws which are immoral. And, as already indicated, the political obligation to obey those laws which are normally wrong, may be overridden by this moral wrongness.

All the claims I make about promising are also true of consenting and agreeing to do something. This is so either because consents and agreements are types of promises or because consenting and agreeing to do something are at any rate like promising in the respects mentioned.

We do not readily speak of tacitly promising to do something. But, as A. John Simmons notes (1979, p. 79) 'genuine instances of tacit consent, at least in non-political contexts, are relatively frequent'. He uses the following illustration (1979, p. 79):

Chairman Jones proposes to his fellow board members that the next board meeting, with mandatory attendance, be next Tuesday instead of Thursday and asks whether there are any objections. In the face of agreement from some and silence from the rest he announces 'OK so we are agreed to meet on Tuesday' and closes the meeting.

Provided certain conditions, to be stated in a moment, are satisfied, silence here amounts to tacit consent to the time of the next meeting.

Such tacit consent, like the express consent of the others, is actual consent. Hence the claims I make above, regarding certain features of promising, apply to tacit consent as much as they do express consent. What does it mean to say that tacit consent is actual consent? I take it 'actual', like 'real', operates here as an excluder (see Austin, 1964). That is, to say such consent is actual is to say that it is not pretended consent, that the claim that the silent board members have consented is not metaphorical nor fictional, etc.

Obviously, we are not tacitly consenting to something every time we are sitting somewhere quietly. So under what conditions can inactive silence be taken as tacit consent? I suggest the following:

(1) The situation is such that consent or dissent by certain persons is required.

(2) Absence of dissent by these persons by a certain time counts as consent.

(3) Dissent is possible for these persons and its expression is not unreasonably difficult.

(4) There are no conditions which defeat the claim that such silence counts as consent.

(5) The potential consenters/dissenters are aware that conditions (1) to (4) obtain.[4]

Conditions (1) to (3) are clearly satisfied in the boardroom case. There is nothing in the example which implies condition (4) is not satisfied and further background circumstances can readily be assumed such that it is satisfied. (For example, it can be assumed that neither the chairman nor anyone else threatened the other board members with harm unless they agree, expressly or tacitly, to the proposed date for the next meeting.) Similarly, there is nothing in the example to imply condition (5) is not satisfied and further circumstances can readily be assumed such that it is satisfied.

I have claimed that a promissory obligation is a (moral) reason for doing the promised action. Following Joseph Raz (1975), I now add that this reason is an exclusionary reason. I shall explain what exclusionary reasons are (see 'Authority' below) and argue that promises and commands — like an order from someone in authority — constitute reasons of this kind.

Authority

Within liberal democratic theory, consent must be the basis of political authority. To spell out the sense of this claim requires a threefold distinction the necessity of which has been pointed out by Hart. He notes (1968, pp. 3–4) that with respect to some social institutions (e.g. punishment or property) we must distinguish between questions of definitions, of justification and of distribution. Raz (1975, p. 64) applies this distinction to the institution of authority and notes that we must answer three distinct questions with respect to it.

(1) What is it to be an authority?
(2) How is authority to be jusitified?
(3) How does one acquire authority?[5]

The concept of authority in the problem of political authority

When I ask what the basis of political authority is, I am concerned with what I call authority-over, rather than with authority-on or authority-with. The distinction between the three types of authority is now widely accepted. Authority-over consists in the right to do certain sorts of things, a right which one has by virtue of a role within a hierarchically organised group. The things one has a right to do include issuing commands, making rules and decisions, granting permissions, giving advice, adjudicating, and speaking on behalf of others. As Raz notes it 'is wrong to regard all of these as commanding' (1979, p. 11). It is still an oversimplification to speak of authority-over as the right to make decisions on behalf of those under authority. Nevertheless, I will usually characterise authority-over in this latter way, partly for the sake of simplicity and partly because it is this right which has as its correlative the obligation of those under authority to comply with the authoritative decisions. Authority-on is detailed and systematic knowledge which is recognised as such by others. Authority-with is readily accepted influence by virtue of leadership qualities or office or expertise.

These characterisations are rough.[6] But they suffice to show

9

that authority-over on the one hand, and authority-on and authority-with on the other, are logically distinct. For example, the permanent head of a university's English department may cease to be an effective scholar and administrator. Hence, he may cease to be an authority and to have authority with those over whom he, nevertheless, still is in authority. His decisions may be ignored most of the time by the other department members and he may put up with this for fear of a showdown. Clearly, it is also possible for some other department member to be both an authority on, say, Shakespeare, and to have authority with his colleagues, yet *ex hypothesi* not be in authority over them. One can have a right to obedience though one does not get it and is an expert on nothing; and one can be an expert and have influence, yet not have a right to obedience.

This, of course, is not to deny that the three kinds of authority are contingently related. Being an authority on something and having authority with people may get one a position of authority over people. And being an authority or being in authority is likely to increase the authority one has with people.

Authority-over is institutionalised authority-with. Authority-with refers to the *fact* of compliance, authority-over to a *right* to compliance. Thus, by creating a structure of authority-over relations, involving rights and obligations which correspond to the authority-with relations in an informal group, one can attempt to create an organisation which survives a partial or total turnover of its members. But just because authority-over is the *formal* counterpart of authority-with, it need not necessarily be accompanied by the latter.

One can, of course, be an authority on politics. Further, it may be appropriate to refer to the influence some politicians have with others in political matters as political authority (authority-with). But, as already noted, it is political authority as authority-over, i.e. as a right to the obedience of one's fellow citizens with their correlative obligation to obey, which is the traditional philosophical problem of political authority.

Some discussions of political authority, however, treat it as if it were an instance of authority-on or authority-with. C.J.Friedrich's repeatedly offered analysis of political authority as the 'capacity for reasoned elaboration' is the best known analysis based on the model of authority-on.[7] The following passage is representative of his writings on political authority:

10

> There are . . . power situations which are distinguished from others by the fact that the wielder of power has the capacity to elaborate what he prefers by reasoning which would seem rational to those who follow him, if time and other circumstances permitted . . . What we are proposing is that this capacity for reasoned elaboration . . . should be designated political authority. (Friedrich, 1972, p. 55.)

In most of his discussions of authority, Friedrich builds up a case for his analysis of authority through 'the teacher, the scholar, the doctor, the lawyer, in short the expert specialist' whose 'authority seems to be derived from . . . superior knowledge, insight or experience' (1972, p.46). It is, therefore, clear that he sees authority, including political authority, as authority-on.

Bentham is a clear example of a writer who sees political authority as authority-with.[8] D.H. Monro attributes to him the view that 'a man has political authority when other men habitually obey him' (1967). The following two quotations from Bentham's writings show that Monro's attribution is justified:

> When a number of persons (who we may style subjects) are supposed to be in a habit of paying obedience to a person, or an assemblage of persons, of a known and certain description (whom we may call governor or governors) such persons altogether (subjects and governors) are said to be in a state of political society. (1973, p. 128.)

> Such of them as are subjects may, accordingly, be said to be in a state of submission, or of subjection, with respect to governors: such as are governors, in a state of authority with respect to subjects. (1973, p. 130, note 17.)

Clearly, to see having political authority as being obeyed habitually is to see it as authority-with rather than as authority-over, i.e. as the fact of being obeyed, rather than as a right to be obeyed.

Since the traditional problem of political authority is that of a state's or government's authority over citizens, and since authority-over is logically distinct from authority-on and authority-with, discussions of political authority which see it as authority-on or authority-with cannot provide an adequate account of political authority. Nor could such discussions provide an adequate answer to the question 'What is the basis of political authority?' for the basis of authority-over is unlikely to be the same as that of authority-on or authority-with.

The distinction between the basis and justification of political authority

I have suggested the following rough analysis of authority-over, including political authority-over: the right to make decisions binding on others in certain areas of conduct, a right one has by virtue of a role within a hierarchically organised group. The correlative of this right to make decisions is the obligation of those under authority to comply with the decisions of the person(s) in authority over them.

With regard to such authority-over, we can (as already noted) ask two further questions:

(1) Is authority-over a good thing in a particular area of human activity, i.e. can it be justified?

(2) If so, what is the basis of authority-over in the particular field of activity?

It is important to realise that these are distinct questions, both of which must be answered. Those who are in favour of one person being in authority over others in academic departments may give roughly utilitarian reasons for this view; for example, they may claim that the existence of such an authority relation increases the efficiency and quality of decision-making of the department. But such a justification, even if true, cannot explain why a particular person has such authority-over. For this we need an answer to the question: what is the basis of authority-over in academic departments? And the *initial* answer must be that this person was appointed according to the rules of the university to which the department belongs.

So the interpretation of the question 'What is the basis of political authority?' offered here is this: what gives one the right to occupy a role of authority-over? This right is distinct from the right to obedience which one has if one does occupy this role. So another way of putting our question is: what gives one the right to hold a position which involves a right to obedience? Whatever gives one such a right is the basis of political authority. Both rights are to be understood as moral rights, since a purely legal answer to the question is not sufficient. (The initial answer to the question 'What is the basis of authority-over?', mentioned in the previous paragraph, cannot be the *final* answer, precisely because a purely legal answer to the question is normatively superficial.) So in asking 'What is the basis of political authority?' I am not asking the second but the third of the three questions which Hart and Raz distinguish. I am not asking whether political authority is *justified* but (if it is) on what basis it is to be distributed to particular individuals (Hart) or how particular individuals (rightfully) acquire it (Raz).[9]

Exclusionary reasons

To have authority over others is to have a right to make decisions which are binding on them. Whenever this right is exercised within the terms of the authority relationship the resulting decision creates a reason for action for those under authority. Following Raz (1975) I regard this reason as an exclusionary reason. In this chapter I have already (see 'Consent') claimed that the reason for action created by a promise is also an exclusionary reason.

I will now present a case for this view, drawing on Raz's work. To make clear what an exclusionary reason is, let me contrast it with a (mere) reason, a conclusive reason and an indefeasible reason for action. An indefeasible reason is one which cannot be overridden by any other reason under any circumstances.[10] A conclusive reason is one which, under given circumstances, is not overridden by any other reason. An exclusionary reason does not outweigh or override other reasons but excludes them from counting in the calculation as to what one ought to do. A (mere) reason figures in the calculation along with others (if there are any) and may outweigh such others but does not exclude them from calculation. In short, a (mere) reason can outweigh other reasons, an exclusionary reason can exclude other existing reasons from being put on the scales of practical reasoning.

Both one's own experience of practical reasoning and the functions of promising and authority-over make it plausible that the reasons for action created by promising and by authoritative decisions create exclusionary reasons, not just (mere) reasons. Consider this case: I promise to lend a book to Jane. When she comes to pick it up, another student, Mary, also turns up and asks for a loan of the book. (It is a text in short supply needed by both for the forth-coming examination.) I know both students well and can predict that somewhat more good would come of lending the book to Mary rather than Jane. Also, I have not quite finished with the book and it is inconvenient (but no more) for me to keep the promise. What decision would I reach and on what grounds? First, in these circumstances I think I ought to keep the promise despite the inconvenience to me and although a little more good would come of lending it to Mary. Second, I would arrive at this decision not by carefully assessing whether the promissory obligation outweighs the inconvenience to me and the somewhat greater good of lending the book to Mary, but rather by thinking that I have bound myself to lend the book to Jane and that the reasons of inconvenience and somewhat greater good, therefore, do not count. Moreover, I suggest, it is precisely one of the functions of promising to create reasons for action which exclude the mere inconvenience of doing the promised action and somewhat greater utility of not doing it from counting against doing the action. This, in part, is what it means to commit oneself to do something.

Analogous remarks apply to the commands of someone in authority. Often persons who are ordered to do something will, as a matter of fact, do the action without deliberating whether the inconvenience of doing it when ordered overrides the reason for action created by the command and without deliberating whether doing some other action at the time will lead to somewhat more good. And, as Raz notes, the co-ordination function of authority-over relations can be achieved only if commands are reasons which exclude some other reasons for action, such as inconvenience and minor loss of utility, from counting in practical reasoning (1975, p. 64).

Two further points are important for understanding exclusionary reasons. First, while an exclusionary reason does exclude some other reasons from counting, it is also a reason for doing something. Second, an exclusionary reason has a particular scope, i.e. though it excludes some kinds of reasons from counting, it does not necessarily exclude all other reasons from doing so (Raz, 1975, p. 46). Raz makes no attempt to state what the exclusionary scope of either the promissory reason or the command reason is. But his own examples of such reasons imply that they exclude at least mere inconvenience and modest loss of utility from counting as reasons against doing a promised or commanded action. And he makes it entirely clear that some moral reasons need not be within the exclusionary scope of an exclusionary reason. Thus he notes that the promise to meet someone may be 'overridden' by the need to take an injured person to the hospital (1975, p. 27, cf. p. 40). And he suggests that if one were commanded to commit an atrocity one ought to refuse, implying, rightly, that a command does not exclude all possible reasons from counting against doing the commanded action. (1975, p. 38).[11]

14

The notion of an exclusionary reason is also useful in explaining what we mean when we speak of being *bound* by a promise or by a decision made by someone in authority or by the result of a vote. By this we cannot mean that a promise etc. creates an indefeasible reason for action. On the other hand to say that a promise creates a (mere) reason for action seems too weak to capture the idea of being bound. To claim that it creates an exclusionary reason seems to capture the idea of being bound very well. If one is bound by a promise one has more than a (mere) reason for action but one may, nevertheless, be morally justified in breaking the promise.

The claim that the agreement to obey the state, which is the basis of political obligation and authority, creates a reason, but not a conclusive reason, for obeying the state, figures prominently in this book. It is essential for the plausibility of consent theory. That this reason for obedience is an exclusionary reason rather than, say, a mere reason of considerable weight, neither helps nor hinders the plausibility of consent theory. Nevertheless, I have included the claim that reasons created by promises and commands of authority are exclusionary reasons for action for two reasons. The claim is extremely plausible and likely to become widely accepted, at least among theorists working within the good reasons approach to practical philosophy. Second, it may *seem* that consent theory is less plausible if the claim mentioned is correct. I wish to show that this is not so.

Obligation, duty and ought

By political obligation I refer to the specific and particular obligation which is the correlative of political authority. To appreciate the plausibility of consent theory it is important to distinguish this obligation from other specific moral reasons one may have for obeying a state, especially what may be called 'natural' obligations or duties and from the claim that (everything considered) one ought to obey the state.

Since most moral and political philosophers have until recently used the terms 'obligation', 'duty' and 'ought' interchangeably and I believe this to be a mistake, I have to explain how I propose to use them.

In the language of rational agents one expects to find resources to express the judgement that one has a reason for doing X and the judgement that one has conclusive reasons for doing X. It is clear that the resources for making this distinction exist in ordinary English. We readily speak of having conflicting obligations. For example, one may have an obligation to tell one's spouse what work one does but also an obligation to one's employer not to do so. One can also have conflicting duties. *Qua* employee it may be my duty to give a lecture but, *qua* parent, to look after my sick offspring. Hence both obligation- and duty-judgements are judgements at the a-reason-for-action level, for one cannot have conclusive reasons to do X and Y, given that they are mutually exclusive. Now, if one asked a friend for advice in one of the conflict situations mentioned, such advice could appropriately be expressed as 'Well, I think you ought to look after your sick son and cancel the lecture'. This illustrates the fact that (unqualified) ought judgements are judgements everything considered, i.e. conclusive-reason-for-action judgements.

The assumption made by most writers until recently that ought-statements, obligation-statements and duty-statements are logically equivalent is clearly false as far as ordinary English is concerned. We make ought-judgements in some spheres where a corresponding obligation- or duty-judgement would be inappropriate. Consider: in glazing a vase it may be the case that I ought to use a darker shade of blue; I think it is the case that I ought to clean my teeth regularly. But it is not my duty to do either of these things nor am I under an obligation to do them. (One could of course have an obligation to do such things, e.g. if one has promised to do them; and it could be one's duty to do them, e.g. if it is one's job in some unusual project to clean one's teeth regularly or to use a certain shade of blue. The point of course is that this need not be so and that these, therefore, are commonly situations where ought-statements do not entail corresponding obligation- or duty-statements.) The ought-statements in these examples are instances of non-moral ought. But there are also moral ought-judgements where the substitution of obligation or duty for ought is at least highly dubious. Consider: I have a ticket for a Kiri Te Kanawa concert but cannot go. I also know a poor student-singer with great talent but without a ticket; she would benefit considerably from hearing and seeing Kiri Te Kanawa in action. Plausibly I *ought* to give her the ticket; but do I have an *obligation* to give it to her unless I have done some special act which created such an obligation (e.g. have promised to give it to her)?[12] Moreover there are some obligation-statements which cannot be fully translated into ought-

16

statements without smuggling in reference to an obligation. 'I have an obligation to Smith to give Jones 50 dollars' is not fully translated by 'I ought to give Jones 50 dollars'. To add 'because I promised Smith to do so' is to smuggle in references to the obligation. In other words: if I have an obligation to do X it can often be asked to whom I have this obligation, but this question is not appropriate in respect of 'I ought to do X'.

We also talk of obligations and duties quite differently in ordinary English. We *do* or *perform* our duties, but *meet* our obligations. We can be *on* or *off* duty, but are *under* obligations. Firms advertise jobs in terms of duties, not obligations, and urge customers to inspect their ware without obligation, not without duty. We can act beyond the call of duty but not beyond the call of obligation (though one can of course do more than one is obligated to do). One can speak of something being one's duty *as a* father or chairperson or citizen, i.e. duties can be tied to roles in a way obligations are not.

Once the assumption that ought-, obligation- and duty-statements are logically equivalent is given up, the following rough analyses of *obligation*, *duty* and *ought* can be seen as not only consistent with the distinctive features of the usage of each, but also as more plausible than any other analyses.

Obligation

A person's obligations arise out of the commitments he makes by way of voluntary acts. The clearest example is of course a promissory obligation. But similarly, to order 30 dollars' worth of groceries is to commit oneself to pay the grocer 30 dollars. And to accept a good deed is to commit oneself to do a good deed in return should the occasion arise.

Duty

A person's duties are determined by the roles he has. Such roles are defined in terms of duties, i.e. in terms of the regular tasks that are to be performed because one has a certain role. E.g. the social role of parent is defined in terms of the tasks one must perform regularly (the duties) with respect to an offspring.

Ought

'A ought to do X' is logically equivalent to 'There are conclusive reasons for A's doing X'.

Such ought- or conclusive- reason-for-action judgements are

17

necessarily made from some point of view. My financial adviser may tell me 'You ought to work harder' (because I am facing bankruptcy and there are good business opportunities), my doctor may tell me 'You ought to take a holiday' (because I'm near total exhaustion), and a friend 'You ought to keep working but less hard' (to take some advantage of the business opportunities but without ruining my health completely). They give different advice and make different ought-judgements because they take different considerations into account: business considerations only, medical considerations only, prudential considerations only (but unlike the financial and medical advisers, the friend takes into account *all* prudential considerations). Yet another friend may tell me 'You ought to get out of your business and do something else' because he considers my business, importing child pornography, morally wrong. Hence his advice is advice from the moral point of view, which takes into account prudential considerations but includes consideration of the welfare of others as well.

It is clear enough that ought-judgements are closely tied to reasons for action. For, if I am told I ought to do X, I can legitimately ask why I ought to do X. And if it really is the case that I ought to do X, then the reason(s) for doing X must be better than the reason(s) for doing any other action. Putting it differently: often an ought-judgement expresses a solution to a practical problem, but for it to be a *solution* it must involve not just *a* reason for doing something but *conclusive* reasons for doing it.[13]

It may be objected that, whatever the plausibility of the proposed analysis of ought-judgements is for *particular* ought-judgements, it cannot be correct for *general* ought-judgements or principles such as 'One ought to keep one's promises'. For, according to the proposed analysis, this general judgement would be logically equivalent to 'An action being one of promise-keeping is a conclusive reason for doing it'. But we know that one can be morally justified in breaking a promise. This objection overlooks the fact that moral principles are defeasible principles in Hart's sense of this expression (Hart, 1963; compare Molnar, 1967). Therefore, 'One ought to keep one's promises' is elliptical for '*normally* an action being one of promise-keeping is a conclusive reason for doing it'. The use of the unqualified statement 'One ought to keeps one's promises' in ordinary practical discourse is not too misleading since circumstances in which an action being one of promise-keeping is not a conclusive reason for doing it are exceptional. Ordinarily, if one has promised to do something, this is a conclusive reason for doing the action, i.e. normally there are no other moral reasons which override the promissory reason.

'There are conclusive reasons for doing X' seems to be an adequate analysis of both particular and general ought-judgements, provided it is recognised that general ought-judgements often express defeasible principles and that every ought-judgement is made from a particular viewpoint (e.g. the medical, financial, prudential, aesthetic or moral point of view). This analysis does justice to the intuition that there are important differences between, say, a moral and a prudential ought-judgement and the further intuition that 'ought' is not indefinitely ambiguous.

Natural and institutional morality

One can create reasons for action from the moral point of view by doing certain voluntary acts, by promising, consenting, agreeing to do something, by accepting help from others, by ordering goods from a store. But there are, of course, also moral reasons for action which are independent of one's past actions. That a person is starving is a moral reason for giving him food even if one has done nothing in the past to commit oneself to help this person. I will call the former part of morality 'institutional' and the latter 'non-institutional' or 'natural'. As previously noted, reasons of institutional morality can exist where without, say, a promise there would have been no moral reason for an action and they can exist in addition to reasons of natural morality, thus reinforcing them. Both types of reasons feed into judgements concerning what, morally speaking, ought to be done in a particular situation.

The characterisations of 'obligation' and 'duty' already given place them in the sphere of institutional morality. We speak of an obligation when we have created a moral reason for action arising out of a voluntary act of commitment and of a duty when we have a moral reason to do something by virtue of a role we occupy. But this leaves no words to express economically and conveniently the judgement that there is a (not necessarily conclusive) moral reason for doing something within the sphere of natural morality. If 'obligation' and 'duty' are restricted to commitments and roles, then we cannot say that we have an obligation or duty to help total strangers simply because without such help they would die. Not surprisingly, many writers have, therefore, resisted the view that obligations and duties presupppose commitments and roles respectively. And it must of course be granted that it has often been said that we have an obligation or a duty to tell the truth or to promote human welfare or to act justly by persons who would deny that such obligations or duties depend on commitments or roles and who have no philosophical or conceptual axe to grind.

If R.B. Brandt's remarks (1964) about the terms 'obligation' and 'duty' are correct then we have an account of their use which does justice to all the points noted. According to Brandt some terms have a paradigm and an extended use. This is so, provided there is a sub-class, within the wider class of all correct uses of a term, which has two features:

> First, members of this sub-class are felt to be especially natural uses of the terms: there is no better word for the occasion and there are no better occasions for the word . . . Second, the contexts in which a given term is felt to be especially appropriate have certain features in common, and the term has come, to some extent, to suggest these features . . . (1964, p. 385).[14]

As Brandt claims, the grammatical features of 'obligation' and 'duty' make it clear that their paradigm uses relate to commitments and roles respectively. But Brandt also acknowledges that there is an extended use of 'obligation' and 'duty' which is independent of commitments and roles. And he suggests that the paradigm uses may be the historically prior ones.

Brandt's suggestion is plausible because there are no words in ordinary English (other than 'obligation' and 'duty') to economically express the judgement 'There is a defeasible reason of natural morality for A to do X'. The need to express such judgements economically has led to the extended use of the words 'obligation' and 'duty'. Indeed, if such an extended use of these words had not already occurred in English, some word would have to be invented to express such judgements of natural morality economically.

Such an extension of use would have been aided by the fact that within the Christian framework, almost universally accepted in past centuries, virtually *all* moral requirements could be seen readily both as obligations *and* duties in the institutional sense of these words. Regarding obligations, this would be the case if one assumes the existence and classical notion of the character of God. God is claimed to have authority over His creatures. Therefore His creatures have an (institutional) obligation to obey Him. God isues the Ten

Commandments to His creatures. Therefore they have an (institutional) obligation not to lie, kill, commit adultery, etc. Another argument can be constructed to show that if God exists, then in our roles as children of God we have a duty to do the things which He, our Heavenly Father, commands us to do. (For the last point see Mothersill, 1967.)

Further plausibility to Brandt's suggestion, as restated and developed a little here, that the use of 'obligation' and 'duty' in the realm of natural morality is an extended and historically more recent one, is lent by the loose use the words have in this realm. For example, while the grammatical differences between 'obligation' and 'duty' make it clear that they cannot be used interchangeably in the realm of institutional morality, they can be used interchangeably in the realm of natural morality. It is linguistically equally appropriate to speak of an obligation or a duty to help people in great need where the requirement is one of *natural* morality. Further, I doubt whether there is a consistent usage of the terms such that we could reportively define the words in terms of certain types of reasons of natural morality. E.g. Is every reason for action within natural morality an obligation/duty? Or is it only the reaching of positive goals (i.e. acts of *commission*) which can be said to be obligations (Brandt, 1964, p. 390)? Or only prohibitions (acts of *omission*) (Mayo, 1958, Chapter XI:)? Or is it only the minimum requirements of natural morality (whether acts of commission or omission) which can be said to be obligations or duties (Fuller, 1976, Hart, 1965)? I doubt whether 'obligation' and 'duty' are used in ordinary English in a way that permits anything other than stipulative answers to these questions.

To present a theory of political obligation within a clear terminological framework, I propose to distinguish between institutional and natural morality as above; to use 'obligation' and 'duty' as part of institutional morality, in the commitment and role sense already presented; to refer to reasons for action of natural morality as *natural* obligations; and (for the sake of simplicity) to call *all* reasons for action of natural morality 'natural obligations'. No arguments will depend on this terminology, nor will it be misleading. To distinguish clearly between a-reason-for-action-judgements and conclusive-reason-for-action-judgements, I will use 'ought' only in the latter sense. Needless to say what one ought to do in a given situation depends on all the reasons for action applicable to the situation, those of institutional and natural morality. Some of these may conflict, in which case the ought-judgement expresses the appropriate

21

weighting of the conflicting reasons.

A few additional remarks may further clarify the moral terminology to be used. There is no need for a *prime facie*/actual terminology with regard to obligations, duties, and oughts commonly used since W.D. Ross introduced it. This terminology is used because writers make both:

(a) the *sound* assumption that we need linguistic means for making the distinction between a reason and a conclusive reason for doing something, and

(b) the *mistaken* assumption that obligation-, duty-, ought-statements are logically equivalent.

The need for the *prima facie*/actual terminology disappears once (b) is abandoned; it disappears once it is realised that ought-, obligation- and duty-statements are not logically equivalent and, moreover, that, at least in their paradigm uses, obligation and duty-statements express a-reason-for-action-statements. Instead of speaking of *prima facie* obligations, *prima facie* duties and *prima facie* oughts, we can simply speak of obligations or duties (including conflicting obligations and duties). Insted of speaking of actual obligations, duties and oughts, we can simply speak of oughts.[15]

I have tried to make remarks about the use of the terms 'obligation', 'duty' and 'ought' which are sufficient to make my use of them clear and to present a clear logical relationship between obligation- and duty-statements on the one hand and ought-statements on the other. As compared to the terminology of most of the recent philosophical literature, the proposed terminology is simpler, but is at least as clear and at least as adequate to the needs of practical discourse. I believe it is also closer to ordinary English than the terminology inspired by Ross. However it is not simply intended to report on correct, ordinary usage. Rather, it tries to extract from ordinary usage a set of (more or less partial) definitions which capture its main tendencies in a way that yields a terminology adequate for practical discourse.[16]

Normative assumptions

Four normative assumptions are starting points in the theory of justified political obedience being developed here. I take for granted the correctness of received moral opinion in claiming:

(1) that people have human (or natural) rights;

(2) that one of these rights is that to personal self-determination;

22

(3) that promises create (institutional or self-assumed) obligations and rights; and

(4) that accepting a good deed puts one under an (institutional or self-assumed) obligation to return a good deed if the need arises.

The first two assumptions are convenient but probably not essential to consent theory. In Chapter 3, consent theory is argued for from the claim that normal adults are capable of and therefore have a human right to personal self-determination. This appears to be the most straightforward argument for the claim that political obligation and authority must be based on actual personal consent. But if there are no human rights, it may still be possible to argue in other ways for the claim that, normally, it is morally wrong to exercise political power over persons, who are capable of personal self-determination, without their consent.

The third of the assumptions is the only one which is essential to the present version of consent theory. If, in promising (or consenting or agreeing) to do X, the promiser did not put himself under an obligation to do X, and did not give the promisee a right to X being done, then the present account of political obligation and of political authority would be fatally undermined. Fortunately, this third assumption is the most secure one. The assumption is not that every society must have the promising institution, but that if a society does have it, then if G promises R to do X, G has an obligation to do X and R a right to X being done.[17] This latter assumption is in accordance with moral commonsense and denied by very few theorists.

There are three reasons why the normative assumptions which are important to the present version of consent theory need not be argued for here. First, a good case for the claims here assumed is already available in the literature. Second, any particular case for these claims, presently available, is likely to be less secure than the claims themselves. Third, especially given the first two reasons, it seems entirely legitimate to present to the reader a work which argues out the *political* aspects of consent theory but takes for granted some plausible and widely held *moral* claims.

In short, the present work makes a case for the plausibility of the conditional claim that if (a) there are human rights and (b) people have the capability of and the human right to personal self-determination and (c) promises create obligation and rights, then actual personal consent must be the basis of political obligation and authority.[18] I make a case for the conditional claim; I assume the antecedent. But, needless to say, I would not assume the three parts of the antecedent if I did not regard them as highly plausible and if they were not widely accepted.

The fourth asumption, that accepting a good deed puts one under a (reciprocal) obligation to return a good deed if the need arises, I make simply because it seems extremely plausible. In the political context, reciprocal obligation can give rise to an obligation to comply with the law, which is distinct from and additional to political obligation, i.e. the obligation to obey the state which is the correlative of political authority. This additional (reciprocal) obligation to obey the law is not an integral part of consent theory and its absence would, therefore, do it no damage.

Notes

1. This list is not meant to be complete; moreover, it may be open-ended in the sense that it may always be possible to discover further types of defeating conditions.

2. Here is an illustration for defence (1d): Jones can save Smith's life at an insignificant cost to Jones, say, by calling an ambulance or by taking Smith to a nearby hospital. But Jones makes his offer to save Smith's life conditional on Smith promising to give Jones 5,000 dollars. The promise would fail to come off even more obviously if the promises were responsible for the predicament of the promisee.

3. The claim that a putative promise fails to come off if any of the defeating conditions listed obtains, is an oversimplification. If condition (2b) or (2c) is discovered to hold some time after a promise has been made, and the promiser declares that he wishes to withdraw from the putative promise, it may be best to say that the putative promise did come off but was anulled or voided by the promiser's declared wish and the discovered condition.

4. For two other statements of the conditions of tacit consent see Hunter (1966, p. 33) and Simmons (1979, pp. 80–1). Simmons also proposes the following condition, not included here: 'the consequences of dissent cannot be extremely detrimental to the potential consenter'. The reason for its omission will become apparent in Chapter 6.

5. When I distinguished between the definition, justification and basis of political authority in my paper 'What is the Basis of Political Authority?', I was unaware that Hart and Raz had already made this distinction in their earlier work.

6. Fur fuller characterisations of the three types of authority see Richard B. Friedman (1973) and E.D. Watt (1982).

7. For other writers who see political authority as authority-on see David R. Bell (1971), Peter Bachrach and Morton S. Baratz (1974, Chapter 2) and David V.J. Bell (1975).

8. David Hume also treats political authority as authority-with, instead of authority-over, in some of his writings (see Stuart Brown, 1974, p. 22).

24

However, Brown expresses this claim in terms of the contrast between *de jure* and *de facto* authority.

9. I stress the present point so much since some writers use 'basis' and 'justification' interchangeably. See for example, Steinberg (1978, p. 135).

10. Reasons called here 'indefeasible' Raz calls 'absolute' (1975, p. 27).

11. Flathman's objections (1980, pp. 110–12, p. 119) to the claim that a command by someone in authority creates an exclusionary reason for action is vitiated by his failure to appreciate that such reasons can have a limited scope of exclusion, i.e. exclude some but not all other reasons from counting.

12. For another case to support the distinction being made see Warnock (1971, p. 94).

13. This ignores the possibility of there being two actions, X and Y, for the doing of which there are equally good reasons. In that case one would judge that the agent ought to do either X or Y, i.e. that there are conclusive reasons for doing one of these two actions in preference to any third action.

14. Compare the distinction developed at length by Finnis (1984, especially pp. 10–11), between central and peripheral cases falling under a concept and the distinction between logically primary and secondary cases which I borrow from D.M. Armstrong (1973) and use later (see Chapter 6).

15. I argue in detail for the claim that the *prima facie*/actual terminology is confused, cumbersome and unnecessary in Beran (1972, pp. 213–6). For the sake of brevity, I ignore, at present, important differences between the way Ross and later writers use the *prima facie*/actual terminology. These differences are stated in the article just referred to. Recently Simmons (1979, p. 24–8) and Searle (1978) have also argued for abandoning this terminology.

16. For similar approaches to conceptual analysis, see Raz (1975, p. 18, p. 31). Finnis (1984, p. 278) and perhaps also von Wright (1964, p. 4–6).

17. Why G and R rather than other letters? Often it is difficult to remember which sides of a relationship letters represent. It may help, therefore, to use letters with a mnemonic value. Here G stands for giver of a promise and R for receiver of it. Elsewhere in the book C stands for Chief and I for Indian, and, later, C stands for coercer and V for victim of coercion.

18. The empirical claim that normal adults have the capability of personal self-determination, included here in the complex antecedent for completeness, will be introduced in the next chapter (see 'Exposition').

3

The Membership Version of
Consent Theory

This chapter sets out and argues for the membership version of consent theory. The exposition is preliminary, being supplemented and qualified over the next three chapters, and fully detailed in the last. The chapter spells out some of the implications of consent theory for secession and indicates the errors which some past versions of the theory have fallen into.

Exposition

That the obligation to obey the state has something to do with the consent of the government is not a novel claim within liberal democratic theory. But in what sense of 'obligation' and of 'consent'? One of the basic aims of this book is to show that there is a sense in which it can plausibly and significantly be claimed that consent must be the basis of political obligation (and authority) within a liberal democratic philosophy. Democratic liberalism assumes, of course, that the state is a useful institution in promoting the interests of its members. It assumes that the state can promote liberty, justice and human welfare.

Democratic liberalism also assumes that biologically normal adults satisfy certain minimal conditions of rationality in belief and action; that they, therefore, have the ability to review their beliefs and goals in the light of reasons, to make decisions appropriate to these beliefs and goals and to act on them in order to influence the way the world goes. Such persons are responsible for what they make of themselves and for what they do to others. Here I follow S.I. Benn, (1982, p. 44).[1] In short, democratic liberalism assumes that biologically normal men and women are capable of personal self-

26

determination and that it is, therefore, appropriate to ascribe to them a moral right of personal self-determination.

In the last paragraph I move from the empirical claim that biologically normal persons are capable of personal self-determination to the normative claim that it is appropriate to ascribe to them a moral right of self-determination. Such a move, though controversial, is sound. But to make an adequate case for it would take us too far into meta-ethics.

Many liberal democratic theorists assume that persons are primarily motivated by enlightened self-interest. This assumption, however, is false and consent theory is better grounded in the more realistic assumption that persons are neither perfectly self-interested nor completely altruistic. People can, and often do, act from the moral point of view, i.e. in a way that takes into account the interests of others as well as their own, even if to do so is, at times, against their long-term self-interest.

It should also be assumed — as it is not by all liberal democratic theorists — that we must distinguish between the two kinds of moral reasons for action noted in Chapter 2. These are reasons which are created by one's voluntary actions and reasons which exist independently of such actions — in short, institutional and natural obligations. This assumption is necessary partly because adequate normative ethics must acknowledge the existence of both types of practical reasons and partly because consent theory is plausible only if it acknowledges both self-assumed and natural obligations to obey the state.

If people have the capability and right of personal self-determination, then they also have the moral capacity to make binding moral agreements with each other. (Compare Riley, 1982, on contract theory's need to develop a theory of moral personality which is consistent with persons making such agreements.) Moreover, if they can act from the moral view point of view, then they can keep their agreements even when this is not in their self-interest.

From the assumption that the state can be useful for the promotion of liberty, justice and welfare and the assumption that there are natural obligations, it follows that there can be natural obligations to obey the state. Moreover, in so far as the state is necessary for the promotion of these values, political authority is morally justified. Chapter 2 distinguishes between the justification and the basis of political authority. It may now be asked: what is the basis, as distinct from justification, of political authority which is consistent with all the assumptions made? Here political authority is understood as authority-over, involves the right to make demands on those under authority, and has as its correlative the obligation of those under it to comply with the demands made. And the basis of political authority is that which gives particular individuals the right to hold the office which carries such authority.

So, what is the basis of political authority and obligation? The answer is, of course, consent. The version of the theory to be developed makes the actual personal consent of those under authority its basis. This claim has to be elaborated by indicating what such consent consists in, what the consenter consents to, who the consenters are, and to whom consent is given.

What does consent consist in?

It consists in accepting membership in the state. This version of consent theory may be called the membership version to distinguish it from two other versions of consent theory to be discussed in Chapter 5. The consent which consists in accepting membership in the state can be express or tacit.

Naturalised citizens consent expressly, in becoming citizens of their new state, to comply with the law of the polity they are joining.

Native-born citizens consent tacitly to obey the law. Their continued residence in the state, when they cease to be political minors and assume full political rights, counts as such tacit consent. This is only so provided that certain conditions are fulfilled — most importantly that there is a generally known convention that such continued residence counts as tacit consent. This does not imply that the conditions which make continued residence count as tacit consent now exist in liberal democracies. Nor does it follow that native-born members of existing liberal democracies tacitly consent to comply with the law. This point will be stated more fully later in this chapter (see 'A conservative confusion'). The idea of a convention to the effect that continued residence in a state counts as tacit consent will be presented more fully in Chapter 7.

The distinction between political minors and adult citizens with full rights and obligations of membership is, of course, already recognised in political practice and theory. The following are among the most obvious differences between political minors and adults. The former do not have the legal right to hold political office; they have neither the legal right nor obligation to take part in the selection of government; they do not have the legal right to leave the state without the consent of their legal guardian; they cannot enter contracts and they cannot marry without the consent of their legal guardian; they cannot sue (their 'next friend' has to do it on their behalf) nor be sued, and if a criminal action is brought against them it is heard in a children's court; they cannot serve on juries; and they are legally compelled to do many things (e.g. to go to school) which adults are not compelled to do. Persons cease to be political minors at some time usually between the ages of 18 and 21, when they become full citizens. As already noted, their acceptance of such full membership in the state can, under certain conditions, amount to tacit consent to obey the state.

Following tradition I have written of consent in the last few paragraphs. But the claim being made is most naturally expressed, as follows, in terms of agreeing to obey the state:

(1) In accepting membership in a rule-governed association one agrees to obey the rules of the association.

(2) In agreeing to obey the rules of an association one assumes an obligation to obey these rules.

(3) The state is a rule-governed association.
Therefore,

(4) In accepting membership in a state one assumes an obligation to obey the law of the state.

Two comments will clarify the claim that, in accepting membership in a state, one agrees to obey the state and, therefore, assumes an obligation to comply with it. First, the relationship between accepting membership in an association and agreeing to obey its rules is not logical, but empirical and normative. There seems to be no self-contradiction in the idea of a chess-club accepting Bobby Fischer as a member even if he refuses to agree to obey the club's rules. However, as a matter of fact, associations (nearly?) always insist on members agreeing to obey their rules. Associations do not often (never?) want particular individuals as members so badly that, as an inducement, they waive the requirement to agree to obey the rules (and the requirement to actually obey most of them most of the time). Moreover, associations are justified in insisting that those who become members of an association agree to obey its rules. It is only fair that those who obtain the benefits of membership also accept its burdens. Needless to say, no state would or should extend membership to an individual without that person accepting an obligation to comply with the law.

Second, I acknowledge that I could present the present version

29

of consent theory more precisely had I done more analytical work on the concepts of *promising, consenting* and *agreeing* to do something. I have confined myself to claiming that promising, consenting and agreeing to do something are alike in that all three types of acts create correlative obligations and rights and to claiming that the present version of consent theory is most naturally stated in terms of *agreeing* to comply with the law of the state in which one accepts membership. I have not done further analytical work on the concepts of *promising, consenting* and *agreeing* to do something, since the most important claim of consent theory is that political obligation and authority must be created by a voluntary act of the individual under political obligation. This being an act, which can create both a moral obligation to comply with the state and the moral right to make binding decisions for the community involved in political authority. Whether this act is most appropriately termed one of promising, agreeing or consenting (or even quasi-consenting) is a significant issue but, nevertheless, only a secondary one.[2] A rose by any other name would smell as sweet.

What does the consenter agree to do?

In accepting membership in a state, the consenter agrees to obey the constitution of the state, officials of the state including the government, provided they hold office constitutionally, and all validly enacted laws. Hence the content of political obligation is this: the obligation to obey the constitution, constitutional governments and valid laws. Richard E. Flathman makes the point that if one consents to something one must have a sufficient idea of what one is consenting to (1972, p. 220–1). Otherwise, one may be acting irresponsibly. What I claim the consenter agrees to, means of course that he will have an obligation to obey laws not yet even thought of when he accepts membership in the state. On the other hand, the constitution places limits on what laws can be created, there is ample scope for morally justified disobedience within consent theory, and it must be open to citizens, except under certain conditions, to abandon their membership of a particular state and, therefore, their political obligation to it.

Who is the consenter?

Each person who is under political obligation must have consented himself, expressly or tacitly. This must be so, since the version of consent theory developed here relies on the model of an actual promise, and only one's own agreement to do something can put one under a promissory obligation to do it.

To whom is consent given?

Or, putting it differently, to whom is fulfilment of one's political obligation owed? Political obligation is the correlative of political authority. Therefore, it is an obligation fulfilment of which is owed to the state. Hence consent, in accepting membership in the state, is given to the state as an artificial person.

It follows from the characterisation of consent just given that states have political authority only over those who have actually personally consented. From this it follows in turn that a state may not have political authority over every person who lives in its territory. It will be useful to employ the term 'authoritative state' for a state which has the consent of, and therefore has political authority over, at least the majority of its citizens.

Consent theory interprets political obligation and the right involved in political authority as moral ones, since they are created by a promise-like act. Therefore, one puts oneself under political obligation and authority by accepting membership in the state, only provided such an act is free from the conditions which prevent a promise from coming off. For example, if citizens remain in a state because those who try to leave are severely penalised or because they have an unrealistically rosy picture of conditions in their state because of a combination of censorship and false propaganda by the government, then their acceptance of (continued) membership in their state does not amount to consent.

Are there any realistic ways of avoiding membership in the state in which one has grown up? Any response to this question must acknowledge that there is no habitable territory left on earth which is not claimed by existing states.

(1) Clearly for some there is the possibility of emigration and change of nationality. The following are less obvious alternatives.

(2) A group of individuals which wishes to leave a state and is

31

territorially concentrated, can do so by secession, i.e. by removing themselves and their territory from the state of which they have hitherto been a part. The seceders could join another state or set up an independent state or a stateless society.

(3) Individuals who have the means to leave their state, but cannot find another society which accepts them, could move to a dissenters' territory, if such territories were created by reducing the territories of existing states. I will return to each of these possibilities below.

Two further possibilities I will mention here briefly.

(4) States already grant some foreigners the status of resident alien. Some do so to considerable numbers. Perhaps resident alien status could also be given to native-born persons who neither wish to accept citizenship nor to emigrate. Such a status would involve fewer obligations but also fewer rights than citizenship. (For a discussion of the desirability of granting resident alien status to some native-born persons see Walzer, 1970, Chapter 5.)

(5) Later in this chapter (see 'Consent theory and secession') I argue for the claim that territorially concentrated groups ought to be permitted to secede, provided certain conditions are satisfied. Must states also permit individual persons or single families to secede from them with their quarter-acre blocks of land? It is difficult to envisage the proper relations between such individual independents and the state which surrounds them. (Compare Nozick, 1974, especially pp. 54–5, p. 287ff.) No doubt every person has a right to sufficient room to live and states are not normally justified in compelling persons to be members of them. But *perhaps* the rights of single individuals or families who wish to leave the state they are in, but are not accepted as immigrants by any other society, are sufficiently satisfied by the created of the dissenters' territories already mentioned. So much for the meaning of consent. From what has already been said, it should also be clear as to what is intended by political obligation. It is that particular obligation to obey the state which is the correlative of political authority.[3] This obligation must be distinguished from other institutional obligations one may have to comply with the state, e.g. an obligation arising from participating in democrative elections.

It must also be distinguished from the possible natural obligation to obey the state due to it being necessary for promoting liberty, justice and human welfare. All of these possible obligations could appropriately be called 'political' obligations. However, for present purposes, the label 'political obligation' is restricted to the obligation

32

which is the correlative of political authority. This use of the term is narrower than that of theorists hostile to consent theory. However it is a use of the term which enables one to claim, plausibly and significantly, that actual personal consent is the basis of political obligation and is, therefore, a use in the consent tradition. No substantive issues are settled by terminological fiat here, for it is, of course, not being claimed that consent is the basis of *every* possible obligation to obey the state.

Both the natural obligation and the consent-based obligation to obey the state are essential to a complete theory of justified political obedience. Consent is a necessary part of such a theory, since no adequate account of the political authority of the state can be given without it. What may be called the moral functions of the state, the promotion of liberty, justice and human welfare, are necessary parts of such a theory; for they explain why people *should* consent to obey the state — if it does indeed promote liberty, justice and welfare — and they point to particularly important reasons (of course there can be others) why people may *want* to consent to obey the state.

As against obligations to obey the state, there can also be obligations to disobey it. Consent theory lends itself especially well to a theory of political disobedience. This is so since it bases political obligation on an agreement to obey the state. Such consent can create only a defeasible, not an indefeasible, reason for obedience. True, this reason is an exclusionary reason. (Chapter 2. See 'Authority'.) But while an exclusionary reason created by consent excludes some reasons for disobedience from counting, it does not exclude all possible moral reasons for disobedience from doing so. Therefore, if a particular law is valid and unjust, a citizen could be under political obligation to obey it and under a natural obligation to disobey it. Everything considered it may then be the case that morally he ought to disobey the law, perhaps even publicly, i.e. as an act of civil disobedience. The relation between political obligation and possible moral reasons for political disobedience will be discussed more fully in Chapter 8.

The foregoing characterisation of consent and obligation in consent theory is intended to show clearly that the consent theory of political obligation and authority is only a fragment, though a substantial one, of a liberal democratic theory of the state. It deals with that moral reason for obeying the state which is involved in the existence of a political authority relation between the state and its citizens. Other issues, such as the functions of the state and natural obligations to obey it, are therefore dealt with in this study only in so far as they are relevant to a clear and persuasive statement and defence of consent theory. The following chapters, especially Chapters 4 and 6, will show that, once the narrow scope of consent theory is appreciated, some of the best-known objections to it lose their persuasiveness.

Argument for consent theory

Democrative liberalism assumes that normal adults have the capability for personal self-determination and that it is, therefore, appropriate to ascribe to them a right of personal self-determination. This right includes the right of political self-determination. From this it follows that no one can have authority, including political authority, over any normal adult without the consent of those under such authority. For if some could have authority over others without their consent, the latter would be in a relationship which is not self-determined. Hence the basis of political authority, within liberal democratic theory, must be the actual personal consent of those under such authority.

It is tempting to make the claim that consent is the basis of authority-over a logical claim. However, I will resist this temptation, partly because I have not found, nor been able to develop, any entirely persuasive arguments for this claim, but more importantly, because such a conceptual victory for consent theory would be a hollow one.

Consider a Platonic theory of political authority. (Or a neo-Platonic one should it be anachronistic to attribute to Plato the concept of authority-over as characterised in this book.) Such a theory claims that statements about the good, including the political good, are objective, that only a small minority in any natural community have the capacity to know the good, that such knowledge of the good, rather than the consent of the governed, is the basis of political authority, and that states ruled by persons who do not know the good are corrupt. (Such a Platonic theory of political authority, unlike that of Friedrich mentioned in the previous chapter, does not run authority-on and authority-over together. For the Platonic claim is that being an authority on the good gives one the right to authority over those who are not.)

I do not know any argument to show that this Platonic use of the concept of authority-over is untenable. But even if this could be shown to be so, a Platonist could surrender the concept of authority-over, yet still maintain the substantive thesis that, given the truth of the claims mentioned, only those who have knowledge of the good have a right to occupy the office of ruler. No purely conceptual thesis can undermine this claim.

Hence, instead of claiming that, according to democratic liberalism, the consent of the governed is a *logically* necessary condition of political authority, I suggest a looser theoretical relation-ship between political authority and its basis. I suggest that 'C is in authority over I' be analysed roughly as 'C has the right to make decisions binding on I in certain areas of conduct, by virtue of the roles which C and I occupy in a hierarchically organised group'. This may roughly be the concept used in ordinary English, and it can be used in a theory-neutral way by conservative, liberal and radical political philosophers. What the basis of political authority is claimed to be, i.e. what is claimed to give one the right to occupy the office of ruler, is not part of the concept of political authority and is not theory-neutral at all. Different assumptions about human nature, the objectivity of value-judgements and other matters, make different claims regarding the basis of political authority appropriate. Within the assumptions of democratice liberalism, however, only the personal consent of the governed can be an appropriate basis of politcal authority.

The last claim can be reinforced by considering the alternative bases for political authority that might be suggested. The following alternatives appear to be exhaustive. The basis of political authority is either something external to the holder of it, or a property of his. External bases could be the rules for conferring authority existing in a society, or, if one goes beyond rules, delegation from above or conferment from below. Alternatively, the basis of political authority may be, not something external to the holder of it, but a property of his.

It should be clear that of these alternatives, the only one consistent with the basic assumptions of democratic liberalism is, ultimately, conferment from below. True, to be in authority over others one must have acquired the position in accordance with the rules of the group. But some writers give the impression that an adequate account of the basis of political authority can be given by pointing to such rules alone, provided that political authority as such is justified. For example, R.S. Peters writes that such rules 'give' those in authority the right to issue orders (1966, p. 238), that this right is 'bestowed' on them by such rules (1968, pp. 86–7), and that such rules 'authorise' those in authority (1969, p. 298). Since Peters has nothing to say on what makes it possible for rules to 'bestow' authority-over, he gives the impression that rules as such can do this. But surely this cannot be so. Especially given the liberal democratic assumption of a right of personal self-determination, rules for conferring authority cannot confer authority if they are not accepted by the group to which they are supposed to apply. On the other hand, it is clear that authority can be bestowed by a group following rules for bestowing authority which they have undertaken to follow.

Authority can be delegated from above (though this raises questions about the basis of the authority of those who do the delegating). The only possible agent who could delegate the authority of governments of the sovereign state is God. However, it is clear that God does not bestow authority on governments. For if He did, He would do so clearly. But there are no clear signs of Him bestowing political authority on particular individuals.

Political authority can be conferred from below by those who are under it. Either an elite or all the adult citizens of the state would have to have the right to take part in the process of conferring political authority from below. It is clear that only the latter alternative is consistent with the liberal democratic assumption that all normal adults have a right of self-determination.

Finally, it may be claimed that some personal property of certain persons is the basis of political authority. Relevent knowledge, restricted to a minority, is the most important candidate. The claim would be that such a personal property in itself gives the bearer the right to political office, irrespective of the existing practice of political authority. Again it must be clear that any such theory of the basis of political authority is inconsistent with the liberal democratic assumption that normal persons are capable of personal self-determination . To make this latter assumption is, of course, *not* to deny that people differ considerably in their abilities, including their political understanding. However, it *is* to assume that the abilities of the less able, biologically normal, adults are still sufficient to permit personal self-determination and, therefore, the ascription to them of a right to determine their political relationships.

It seems reasonable to conclude, therefore, that within liberal democratic assumptions, only the individual consent of the governed is a plausible candidate for the basis of political authority.

Consent theory and secession

If people have a right of personal and, therefore, political self-determination, then the basis of political authority must be consent. The possibility of such consent-based political authority is much increased if territorially concentrated minorities which do not wish to be part of an existing state are allowed to secede.

Liberal democratic theory is committed to the permissibility of secession quite independently of its desirability in order to increase the possibility of consent-based political authority. The claim is this: if persons have a right of personal and political self-determination, then secession must be permitted if it is effectively desired by a territorially concentrated group and if it is morally and practically possible.[4] This is required by the value democratic liberalism places on freedom, by a liberal democratic theory of popular sovereignty and by a presupposition of legitimate majority rule.

Freedom

From the claim that adults have a right of personal self-determination it follows that individual freedom is a basic value of democratic liberalism. For such freedom is required for developing and exercising the capacity for personal self-determination. In turn it follows that liberal democrats see the ideal society as one that comes 'as close as a society can to being a voluntary scheme' (Rawls, 1971, p. 13). This does not mean that in a liberal democratic state there are no constraints on those who wish to interfere with the freedom of others. But it does mean that all relationships among sane adults in such a society should be voluntary. In societies imbued with liberal principles this view is embodied with some consistency. In contemporary liberal democracies one's relationships with adults — marital, work, political — are voluntary. In such societies one's marriage partner is chosen by oneself, not one's parents; one chooses or achieves one's employment status, one is not born to it; and governments are chosen in elections from candidates who offer themselves for office. Nor are such relationships, once entered, irrevocable. Divorce is permitted, employment relationships can be terminated, governments can be voted out of office. Moreover, the relationship between the individual adult citizen and the consistently liberal democratic state is voluntary, since such citizens have the right to emigrate and change their nationality.

37

One area to which the idea of the voluntariness of human relationships has not been applied by democratic liberalism, in theory or practice, is that of the unity of the state itself. Yet it seems that a commitment to the freedom of self-governing choosers to live in societies that approach as closely as possible to voluntary schemes, requires that the unity of the state itself be voluntary and, therefore, that secession be permitted where possible. No less than this is implied by one of the very few statements by a liberal democratic philosopher that can be found in print on what legitimates the unity of the state, though the implication is not noted by the author. I have in mind the following remarks by Carl Cohen on the liberal democratic community:

> No such community can be based on force. By force a collection of persons may be coerced . . . into obedience; by force they may be frightened into seeking community for protection. But the nature of genuine civil community is such that force cannot be the principle of unity. That unity must be founded on consent . . . (1971, p. 44).

If people have a right of individual self-determination, then this consent must, of course, be that of the present citizens of the state.

Sovereignty

According to democratic liberalism the citizens have political sovereignty. This must be so if they have a right of personal self-determination. Since such a political philosophy is an individualist one, the sovereignty of the people cannot be an essentially collective property which can only be exercised by all the citizens of an existing state within eternally immutable borders. Instead, this sovereignty must be composed of the moral rights of individuals to decide their political relationships. Democratic liberalism grants this for individual citizens by acknowledging their right to emigrate and to change their nationality. Democratic liberalism must also grant that territorially concentrated groups can exercise their sovereignty, i.e. their moral right to determine their political relationships, through secession rather than mass emigration. It must grant this if we assume, quite reasonably, that a group of people who have traditionally occupied an area have a right to continue to occupy it. But, anyhow, the whole of the habitable earth is now under the

jurisdiction of existing states and a territorially concentrated group
which wishes to leave its state can, therefore, do so much more
readily by secession than by mass emigration. In short, individualist
democratic liberalism must give an individualist interpretation of
the sovereignty of the people.

Majority rule

If people have a right of political self-determination, then, given
that they are united in a polity, they must also have the right to
determine which of the types of political decisions that have to be
made are made by majority vote of all citizens. But we must
distinguish between two kinds of decisions a group may make:
decisions on what rules an association should have, given that a
group of people do want to be one association, and the decision
whether a group do want to be one association. The second type
of decision cannot always be made in a morally binding way by
majority vote among *all* group members. It follows from the value
liberal democrats place on liberty and from a liberal democratic
account of popular sovereignty that, if there are separatists, they
should be permitted to specify the territory of the state in which
a secessionist referendum is to be held. (This claim will be developed
and qualified below.) For, if all citizens of the existing state could
vote in the referendum, they could outvote the separatists; and if
the existing central government used such a vote as a basis for
preventing secession by force, the unity of the state would not be
voluntary, nor would the separatists be able to exercise their share
of political sovereignty — their right to determine their political
relationships.

There is an argument for the claim that separatists should be
permitted to specify the territory in which the secessionist referendum is held, an argument independent of those from liberty and
sovereignty. There appear to be only two ways in which a majority
vote can yield a moral reason for accepting the outcome of the vote.
First, if a group of people agree to settle an issue by a majority vote,
this agreement creates a moral reason for accepting the outcome
for all parties to the agreement, whether they vote with or against
the majority or abstain. But, second, there may be circumstances
in which the fact that a decision has been made by majority vote
creates a moral reason for accepting the decision even for those who
do not agree that a decision be made in this way. This may be so if:

(1) there is a group of people none of whom can leave the group;

(2) a decision binding on all group members must be made; and

(3) a majority vote is a fair procedure for making the decision. Assume that these conditions are satisfied if there is an infectious, dangerous, but curable disease among a group of people marooned on a small island. Assume further that a procedure for dealing with the disease is adopted by majority vote but that a minority refuses to make the decision in this way and boycotts the vote. It seems plausible that, under these circumstances, there is a moral reason for the dissenters to follow the procedure adopted by the majority vote and this is so because it was adopted in this way. But even if there is such a second way in which a majority vote can create a reason for accepting its outcome, it is clear that this way often does not apply to separatist situations. For often in such situations, condition (1) is not satisfied, i.e. the dissenters can remove themselves from the larger group by secession.

Hence, in those cases where separatists can leave an existing group, the use of the majority principle creates a moral reason for their accepting the outcome of a vote only if they have given their agreement as to who is permitted to have a vote in the secessionist referendum. And normally, of course, they would insist that the franchise be restricted to the residents of a territory in which they have some prospect of achieving a majority for secession.

It will be useful to indicate how the majority principle can be used to determine the people/territory which should be allowed to secede and to provide a list of some of the conditions which may make secession morally or practically impossible. The majority principle could be used easily enough to determine whether a people/territory will be permitted to secede if the territory in question can be specified independently of the majority principle, e.g. as a particular province of a federal state or as the territory traditionally occupied by a nation (in the cultural sense) within a multinational state. But I am claiming that *any* territorially concentrated group is a potential candidate for permissible secession. So how can we determine whether secession should be permitted? This can be done by permitting separatists to specify the territory which is to be a candidate for secession and using the majority principle 'recursively' to determine which, if any, territory ought to be permitted to secede.

This is how the idea could be applied. Let the separatists specify the area in which a plebiscite is to be held, e.g. North Wysteria. Assume there is a majority for secession and that secession is granted

in principle. Now any area of North Wysteria must in turn be permitted to vote on whether it wishes to secede from North Wysteria
(and stay with what is left of Wysteria, if they wish). If the majority
of, say, North West Wysterians does not wish to be part of the
independent state of North Wysteria, any region of North West
Wysteria could in turn vote whether to secede from North West
Wysteria etc.

This 'recursive' use of the majority principle over any territory
specified by separatists must give a determinate and consistent result.
It does not give rise to a vicious regress. The regress is not vicious
logically, since it cannot proceed beyond a two-person policy. Nor
is it vicious practically. What little evidence there is on secession
does not support what has recently been called the 'domino theory
of secession', i.e. the claim that an initial successful secession is likely
to lead to a series of secessions resulting in unviable political entities
(see Onyeonoro S. Kamanu, 1974). A number of legal non-colonial
secessions have occurred in the twentieth century. For example,
Norway seceded from Sweden in 1905 and Iceland from Denmark
in 1944. These secessions were not followed by further secessions
from the newly independent or the parent states. It must, of course,
be granted that a more liberal attitude towards secession than has
existed up to now is likely to lead to a greater number of secessions
taking place. But there is little reason to assume that such an
attitude would lead to many unviably-sized political entities. For
people do not disrupt the unity of an existing state lightly, especially
if it is not in their self-interest and if the grievances which make
secession appealing to them are dealt with fairly and sympathetically.
Moreover, political separation at one level can go hand in hand with
economic (and political) integration at another. The Basques
could secede from Spain while also, with Spain, joining the EEC.[5]
At any rate, the fear of Balkanization may be largely illusory. For
R.A. Dahl and E.R. Tufte have shown that there is no significant
relationship between the size of states and either their GNP *per
capita* or their ability to survive as politically independent entities
(1973).

Democratic liberalism is committed to the view that any territorially concentrated group within a state should be permitted to
secede if it wants to and if it is morally and practically possible.
A complete specification of the conditions which make secession
impossible is beyond the scope of this book; it may not be possible
at all. Still, some conditions can be suggested. The conditions which
may justify *not* allowing secession could include the following.

(1) The group which wishes to secede is not sufficiently large to assume the basic responsibilities of an independent state.

(2) It is not prepared to permit sub-groups within itself to secede although such secession is possible.

(3) It wishes to exploit or oppress a sub-group within itself which cannot secede in turn because of territorial dispersal or other reasons.

(4) It occupies an area not on the borders of the existing state so that secesssion would create an enclave.

(5) It occupies an area which is culturally, economically or militarily essential to the existing state.

(6) It occupies an area which has a disproportionally high share of the economic resources of the existing state.

However, the last three of these conditions need not be insuperable barriers to secession. The viability of an enclave depends largely on the goodwill of its immediate neighbour. It may be unjust to withhold such goodwill. Some territorial difficulties can be overcome by the resettlement of people, if they consent and receive appropriate compensation. The need for some control over territory for cultural, military or economic reasons may be satisfied through joint legal sovereignty over it or an appropriate bilateral treaty. Some economic problems may be solvable by compensation payments by the secessionists to the parent state for the disproportional share of economic resources lost to the latter; or by joint ownership of resources in the secessionist state, by it and the parent state or their citizens.

Errors avoided

The present theory tries to avoid some errors of past versions of consent or contract theory. Mention of the most important of these will serve to explain why the present version of the theory takes the shape it does.

Rousseau's riddle

Consent theory must pose the theoretical problem it attempts to solve in a way that permits a solution. Rousseau, in trying to describe a state in which 'each associate . . ., while uniting himself with all may still obey himself alone' (*The Social Contract*, Book 1, Chapter VI) fails to do this. As long as people disagree on what ought to be done, those who wish to live in polities must be prepared to obey others to some extent. They must accept that there are some kinds of issues on which governments have the right to implement the will of the majority. To this extent it cannot be the case that each citizen obeys himself alone. Of course, the present version of consent theory limits this element of heteronomy in two ways. First, the requirement to obey the will of others is normally a moral one only if the citizen, by accepting membership in the state, has agreed to be bound by the majority rule. Second, the resulting obligation to accept the majority will can be overridden by other moral considerations. Hence, if the majority decision is morally iniquitous, citizens may be morally justified in defying the majority.

What Rousseau writes (in Chapter VII and elsewhere) in *The Social Contract* can be interpreted as a solution of the problem quoted above, along the following lines. The state, to be legitimate, must legislate by means of universal participatory democracy. Therefore, every citizen has the right to take part in making the laws which he has to obey. Each citizen may have a private will (the pursuit of his particular interest) and a general will (the pursuit of the common interest). The general will of the legislative body is not necessarily the will of all nor the will of the majority,. Rather it is the will of the legislative, provided certain conditions are met, most importantly these: each citizen tries to decide what is in the general interest, there is adequate debate of the issue to be decided, and the perception of what is in the general interest is not distorted by the existence of and participation in debate of factions. If all the relevant conditions are met, then the legislative decision expresses the general will of the legislative and any minority that voted against the successful resolution fails to express the general will. Hence if they are forced to comply with the decision made they are forced to comply with the general will, which includes *their* general will, their proper will as citizens. Hence in being forced to obey the general will they are obeying themselves alone in the sense that, while admittedly not obeying their private will, they are obeying their general will.

Rousseau's solution fails because it assumes that there are objective normative truths and that the majority of legislators will always vote for legislation in accordance with these truths, if the conditions mentioned are met. But even if the first assumption is correct, there are no good reasons to believe the second one is. Human beings and their institutions certainly can be improved. But we are a very long way from infallible majorities. But if the majority fails to vote in the general interest, then in Rousseau's own terms it is not the case that the minority, in being made to comply, is obeying its own general will; hence the members of the minority would not be obeying themselves alone.

Even if citizens and their institutions could be improved so that majorities did always adopt resolutions which are more in the general interest than any other resolutions before them, it is excessively utopian to assume there could be no informed yet honest disagreement as to whether the resolution adopted was the correct one. Surely some in the defeated minority could, at times, honestly believe, even after full debate, that the majority had erred. If they are forced to comply with the majority decision they are made to comply with a law which, is, *ex hypothesi*, in the general interest. But there is no legitimate sense of 'will' in which they are obeying their own will alone in such cases.

The problem, of which consent theory is the solution, may be posed as follows. Given that the state, and therefore political authority, is *justified* and that people have a moral right of personal self-determination, what can be the *basis* of political authority and of the correlative political obligation? And given the answer that only actual personal consent can be such a basis, what form must such consent take in theory, and is such consent based political authority possible in practice?

Hobbes's howler

Consent theory must take a sufficiently optimistic view of human nature and the circumstances people find themselves in, to give self-assumed reasons for political obedience a significant place in a theory of justified political obedience. Hobbes's version of the theory fails to do this. Of course, Hobbes asserts that there is 'no obligation on any man which arises not from some act of his own' (*Leviathan*, Part II, Chapter 21) and that political authority requires an act of authorisation by the governed (see Gauthier, 1969, Part IV). But he takes such a pessimistic view of the human condition that he also asserts that rulers must be given absolute and undivided political power and that rulers who manage to maintain themselves in power must be obeyed no matter how oppressive they are. This, according to Hobbes, is so since the attempt to overthrow rulers is likely to return the governed to the calamitous state of nature and any government is better than that. This means that Hobbes's claims about consent-based obligation and authority operate at a conceptual level only and play no significant role in his theory of justified political obedience. True, according to him, only rulers who have been authorised by the governed to rule have political authority. But Hobbes is committed to the view that, as long as rulers keep the governed out of the state of nature, they ought to be obeyed whether they have been authorised to govern or not.

A more optimistic view of the human condition makes it possible to advance (a substantial fragment of) a theory of justified political obedience in which consent does make a difference as to whether obedience is morally required.

Locke's lacuna

Consent theory has to provide sufficient detail about the consent which it claims is the basis of political obligation and authority. Notoriously, Hobbes, Locke and Rousseau fail to do so. One of the main aims of this book is to develop a version of consent theory which provides an account of consent which is clear and adequately detailed. It expounds a version of the theory which appeals to actual personal consent rather than to hypothetical or original consent. The reasons for adopting actual rather than hypothetical consent are given in the next chapter. Original consent or contract must, of course, be rejected as a theoretical option because only a person's own promise can bind that person.

Appeal to an original contract is alien to a political philosophy which assumes persons to be capable of personal self-determination and, therefore, to have a right of personal self-determination. Such a philosophy, moreover, has to acknowledge that consent-based political authority relations become possible only once people understand that political authority over such persons must be based on consent. (This point will be stated more fully in Chapter 7.) Thus, the present version of consent theory is entirely consistent with the view, whatever its plausibility, that the state has everywhere come into existence by force. It is committed only to the claim that if people have a right of personal self-determination, then the *authoritative* state can come about only through the actual personal consent of citizens.

The present version of consent theory is constructed to fit naturally the typical person faced with the issue of political obligation and authority. This is the person born into a state which is a going concern. Most citizens of most liberal democracies most of the time wish to maintain their states as such going concerns. The fundamental political question for any given citizen, and the fundamental political consent, is, therefore, whether to (continue to) accept membership in this going concern. Still, new states can and do come into existence through the revolutionary replacement of one political system by another or through a separatist transformation of one state into two. In identifying consent with acceptance of membership in the state the present version of consent theory also provides an adequate account of political authority in such cases.

Johnson's jumble

Consent theory must rely on a kind of consent which can generate political obligation and authority. Karen Johnson (1975) offers an account of political obligation as self-assumed which fails to do this.

It is necessary to distinguish between two kinds of commitment. One can commit oneself to a life of artistic activity and one can commit oneself to lend a neighbour 500 dollars in a week's time. The first kind of commitment is a *resolution* to value certain things and activities and to act in certain ways. Like a New Year resolution it is not essentially social — one can make it while alone — and need not express it to others, though one's actions may indicate what one has resolved to do. The second kind of commitment is an act of *binding oneself to others* to do certain acts (of commission or omission). Thus in promising to do something one commits oneself to do it; in accepting the delivery of goods that one has ordered, one commits oneself to pay the bill; and in casting a vote, one commits oneself to accept the outcome of the election. Such commitments are essentially social, since they are commitments to others that one will do certain things. The first kind of commitment does not create an obligation or a right, the second does. The first kind of commitment may be called a resolution-commitment, the second a right-creating-commitment.

The distinction between the two kinds of commitment may be partly obscured if one's resolution-commitment requires one to do something morally desirable and one joins an organisation which pursues this desirable end. Mother Teresa's resolution-commitment to help the poor does not put her under an obligation to do so. (She and we, of course, may have a natural obligation to help the poor quite independently of any resolution to help them.) But her right-creating-commitment to others to work with them to alleviate poverty does create an obligation to these others to do so.

The consent on which political obligation must be based involves a right-creating-commitment. Persons who accept membership in a state may also have a resolution-commitment to this state. But this is distinct from the right-creating-commitment, and the latter can exist without the former.

Johnson's account of self-assumed political obligation is given by means of a resolution-commitment. She treats political obligation as a moral obligation and distinguishes between a narrow sense of the term, in which it refers to the obligation to obey the law, and a wide sense, in which it refers to a concern for the common good of the members of society. Political obligation as such a concern can require obeying the law but also disobeying it if this is required by the common good. She grants that consent theory is right in claiming that membership in the state and political obligation must be self-assumed. But she also asserts that the state, for its native-born members, is not, and should not be, a voluntary association and that, therefore, such self-assumption cannot be via an act of joining the state. Instead, she claims, the self-assumption of membership and political obligation consists in a recognition that one is a member. Johnson makes it clear enough what this recognition consists in. It is not one's recognition that the state or other citizens regard one as a member. Rather, it is one's own regarding oneself as a member. This involves making the goals and ideals of the state one's own. It involves a commitment to the society into which one was born. As Johnson states: '(i)t might be useful to think of membership from the internal point of view as a continuum, from near-total apathy at one end to near-total commitment at the other' (1975, p. 28). It is clear that the commitment referred to here is commitment as a resolution, not commitment to others which gives these others rights.

Johnson's account of self-assumed membership of the state and of political obligation is incomplete, even in its most obvious essentials, and too limited in scope. Among those who are legally citizens of a state, she distinguishes between those who recognise their membership, those who neither recognise nor reject their membership (cf. the continuum mentioned in the previous paragraph), and those who 'specifically reject membership'. Only regarding those who neither recognise nor reject their membership does she state her position clearly.

They must obey the law, in so far as anyone within the jurisdiction of the state must obey it . . . They are not entitled, just because they do not recognise their membership, to ride free. But theirs is a minimal obligation. They do not have the specifically political obligation which comes with the acceptance of responsibility to have a care for the common good (1975, p. 28).

In short, people who neither recognise nor reject membership are under political obligation in the narrow sense (distinguished above). Those who recognise their membership presumably are under a 'self-assumed' political obligation in the wide sense. Regarding the third lot, those who 'specifically reject membership' and 'choose psychological withdrawal' from the state (1975, p. 29), Johnson is not clear. She writes that she does not see how these people 'can be held to account for a lack of civic virtue' and that they have a 'right to make' their psychological withdrawal (1975, p. 29). She also makes the, presumably, *factual* statement that such an 'individual rejects political obligation', but she does not make the *normative* statement that such an individual has no political obligation.

Johnson's position seems to be that those who commit themselves to membership have political obligation in the wide sense. This, presumably, includes a qualified political obligation in the narrow sense. For a commitment to care for the common good must include a commitment to obey the law as far as this is necessary for the common good. Those who neither recognise nor reject membership have political obligation only in the narrow sense. Those who reject membership presumably do not have political obligation in the wide sense, since not even the uncommitted have it. Johnson gives us no clue whether they have political obligation in the narrow sense. But if those who neither recognise nor reject their membership are not entitled to be free riders regarding obeying the law (political obligation in the narrow sense), then it is not clear why those who reject membership by choosing psychological withdrawal or internal emigration should be allowed to be free riders in this respect. So at best, according to Johnson, it seems political obligation is self-assumed only in the wide sense in which it is an obligation to care for the common good. In the narrow sense of an obligation to obey the law, people have political obligation whether they commit themselves to membership or not. In short, because Johnson rejects voluntary membership of the state, she has left herself with very little scope for self-assumed political obligation.

As well, there is a deeper objection to Johnson's approach because it bases a moral obligation on a resolution-commitment. Common moral opinion does not endorse the claim that such commitments create moral obligations. Johnson gives no argument to show that they do. Nor is there a moral philosophy which makes an adequate case for the view that they do. (Johnson refers to none.) It is true that it may also be claimed that there is no adequate philosophical account of how commitments to others, such as promises, create obligations and rights. But common moral opinion does at least endorse the claim that they do and does so resoundingly.

What the basis of political authority is, Johnson does not consider at all. It is unclear how her account of self-assumed obligation is to be related to an account of the basis of political authority.

A conservative confusion

Consent theorists must not take it for granted that existing liberal democracies (or any other existing states) have political authority (see Chapter 6). They, therefore, must not confine themselves to finding or assuming some consent which accounts for such assumed authority. Instead, they must open-mindedly enquire what kind of consent could be the basis of political authority and explore under what conditions such consent would exist. As stated before, (a) only actual personal consent can provide such a basis; (b) such consent must be understood as a type of promise or agreement; (c) such an act only comes off if it is free from the conditions which prevent it from coming off.

This book makes no pronouncements about the nature of political ties between existing liberal democratic states and their citizens. It seeks to make plausible the claim that *in theory* only consent-based political obligation and authority is consistent with liberal democratic assumptions about human nature. It is desirable to separate the construction of a theory of political obligation and authority from its application to political reality for at least two reasons. First, we have no pre-theoretical beliefs on the possible authority-relation between liberal democratic states and their citizens which are so secure that it is a condition of the correctness of a theory of political obligation and authority that it be consistent with them. Second, if actual consent is a necessary condition of political obligation and authority, then a great deal of empirical information has to be gathered to establish to what extent such consent exists, especially if most of it is tacit. This would require information about citizens and their governments the collection of which is beyond the scope of this study.

To refer to the two approaches to theorising about consent and political authority distinguished above I coin two terms. Versions of consent theory which assume that at least some existing liberal democracies have political authority are referred to as *status quo* versions and those which do not make this assumption as *reform* versions. A reform version does not deny the existence of political authority in liberal democracies; it merely leaves this issue open.

The reform version obviously side-steps one of the most common objections to consent theory, viz. that which points to the dearth of people in existing states who can plausibly be claimed to have actually consented to the political arrangements of their states in a way that would place them under political obligation and authority.

One may be disappointed in a version of consent theory which does not guarantee that at least some existing liberal democracies are authoritative states. If it does not, is such a theory worth developing? It is for at least two reasons. First, the claim that a particular liberal democracy is an authoritative state cannot be assessed without an adequate theory of political authority. Second, even if, in the light of such a theory, it has to be said that no existing state is authoritative, it is important to know what conditions a state must satisfy to be authoritative. For, any group of people who have a right of personal self-determination and believe this to be so and who also believe the state to be a desirable institution will prefer a state which is authoritative to one that is not. Or, putting it differently, they will try to create political institutions which yield decisions which all members of the polity are obligated to obey.[6]

Hobbes's second howler

Distinguishing the membership version of consent theory from what David Gauthier (1976–7) has called 'radical contractarianism', will make clear that it is not open to the same objections. Radical contractarianism is the most extreme version of contract theory yet formulated. Gauthier attributes it to Hobbes and distinguishes it from 'less embracing' versions, such as Locke's.

Gauthier characterises radical contractarianism as follows:

(a) It sees all social relationships, except hostility in the state of nature, as contractual.

50

(b) Because of this, the only standard of rationality is the satisfaction of self-interest.

(c) Since all social relationships are seen as conventional, not only the state but also society is a contractual relationship. This in turn means that persons in the pre-social state of nature must be conceptualised as having the abilities needed for entering a social contract. This must include rationality, language and morality sufficient for this purpose.

The instrumental value of society and the state can be especially easily explained by the assumption that humans are by nature appropriators. Society facilitates co-operation in the production of property, which, relative to the desire for it, is always scarce. The state is needed to enforce contracts on those who wish to and could break them to maximise their self-interest.

As already noted, Gauthier distinguishes radical contractarianism from less embracing forms. These can differ from the radical version thus:

(a) They can assume moral standards which are independent of self-assumed obligations. These standards require humans to relate to each other in ways independent of their self-assumed obligations. The role of the latter, according to less embracing contractarians, is to supplement and complete our natural moral relationships.

(b) The existence of moral standards independent of human agreements makes it possible for rationality to have a standard other than enlightened self-interest. It makes it possible for it to be rational to act benevolently.

(c) Less embracing contractarians do not assert that society is a purely contractual relationship; in other words, they do not advance a social but rather a political contract theory. Therefore, they do not have to conceptualise pre-social persons at all, let alone as having the abilities needed to contract from a pre-social into a social state.

Gauthier claims that, while radical contractarianism is theoretically coherent, it is practically incoherent. By this he means that a society, whose members have, and are fully conscious of having, a radically contractarian ideology, will collapse into competitive chaos. Real men and women who act on such an ideology would need the Hobbesian sovereign to keep them from a war of all against all, but he is not available.

Gauthier introduces the characterisation of radical contractarianism, and distinguishes it from less embracing forms, not only to try to show its practical incoherence, but also because he believes the ideology of Western societies is developing towards radical contractarianism. Few would deny that the ideology of Western societies has been moving and continues to move towards a more contractarian one: from status to contract. But Gauthier claims explicitly 'that our Society is moving towards a more Hobbist position' rather than merely towards a more Lockian one (1976–7, p. 161). The evidence he gives for this claim is not only excessively brief and superficial, but most of it is not evidence at all for a move towards a radical rather than a less embracing form of contractarianism. For example, he claims that the 'rejection by the young of America's role in the Vietnam War and the emergence of radical feminism are manifestations' of an increasingly overt contractarian consciousness from which other motives, such as patriotism and love, are expunged (1976–7, p. 161). But criticism of America's role in the Vietnam War and of the patriarchial family was and is based by very many, and certainly can be based, on a standard of justice which is not contractual. Less embracing forms of contractarianism are entirely consistent with the acknowledgement of love of country and love of people as important motivations in life. They are among the best reasons for voluntarily entering political and marital relationships.

The position advanced in this book is clearly a less embracing form of contractarianism than Hobbes's. My position assumes the existence of natural as well as self-assumed obligations and indicates why both are essential in an adequate theory of justified political obedience. I assume that people can, and often do, act from the moral point of view, i.e. from a point of view which assigns independent value both to the agent's interests and to those of others. The present version of consent theory can distinguish between society and the state and is not committed to a contractarian account of society. The theory is a consent theory not a social contract theory. The theory is committed to the view that *all* authority-over relations among adults must be based on consent, but not to the view that there are no moral relations among people other than voluntary ones. Consequently, while the theory is an individualist one, it is an instance of 'social' rather than 'abstract' or 'radical' individualism.[7] That is, it does not have to ascribe features to pre-social human nature, which humans can develop only in society. Indeed it can insist (a) that humans are essentially social in that they can develop their humanness only in society and (b) that, as a matter of fact, each individual is to some extent the product of his social

52

upbringing. These two assertions are not in conflict with the individualist claim that people have a right of personal self-determination.
For, growing up in a democratic society can help people realise the
very capability of personal self-determination, including the ability
to form sensible voluntary relations, which justifies ascribing to them
a right of personal self-determination.

Two remarks

Consent and different ideologies

Consent theory is here presented within the framework of liberal
democratic philosophy. But the importance of consent-based political
relations is not confined to such a philosophy. The argument for
consent theory, presented above, acknowledges that some political
philosophies can consistently reject the claim that consent must be
the basis of political authority and obligation. (This can be done
consistently, but not plausibly, since such rejection requires making
claims which are false or at least highly implausible.) Still, the claim
that normal persons have the capability for personal self-
determination is not confined to liberal democratic philosophy; and
any other political philosophy which accepts this claim and the claim
that political authority is justified, has to accept consent theory.
Consider, for example, three versions of socialist theory. Anarchists
accept that persons are capable of personal self-determination but,
of course, reject the claim that political authority (the state) is a
morally justifiable institution. Marxist-Leninists accept the need
for the state, during the dictatorship of the proletariat. But their
theory of political authority is perhaps best presented as a Plato-
like epistemological elitism: as the claim that only the vanguard of
the proletariat have sufficient knowledge of the truths of Marxism
and that this knowledge is the basis of their political authority over
those still suffering from false consciousness. However, socialist
theorists who accept both the need for the state and the claim that
normal adults are here and now capable of personal self-
determination have to incorporate some version of consent theory
into their political philosophy. The version of socialist theory which
has to do this involves the social (as distinct from abstract or radical)
individualism sketched in the previous paragraph. It must reject
the extreme collectivism asserted by some socialist theorists but

can also reject the extreme individualism asserted by some liberal and libertarian theorists.[8]

Terminological notes

In the following chapters, 'consent theory' will sometimes refer to the version of theory developed in this book, sometimes to the versions of other writers, and sometimes to consent theory in general. Where appropriate, I will make it clear which of these references is intended.

Earlier in this chapter, 'political obligation' (and actual consent theory in general) is said to refer to that obligation which is the correlative of political authority. Some writers who reject consent theory use the term in other and wider senses. Where (especially in Chapter 4) theories of political obligation are referred to which use the term in a wider sense, this is made clear.

Notes

1. Benn's is a particularly powerful statement of the optimistic view of human nature which is central to a liberal democratic philosophy. For an extended exposition of this view, see Gaus (1983).

2. The term 'quasi-consent' is introduced by Peter Singer (1973, p. 47) to distinguish a particular type of voluntary act which creates an obligation from both express and tacit consent. The latter two, according to Singer, are instances of actual consent, while quasi-consent is not. Singer writes that the obligation created by the voluntary act which is not actual consent 'depends on the fact that under certain circumstances, actions or failures to act may justify us in holding a person to be obliged *as if* he had consented, whether or not he actually has'. This Singer calls 'quasi-consent', 'the prefix indicating that it is not real consent, but gives rise to obligations as if it were real consent' (1973), p. 47). Singer's examples of quasi-consent include the following: participating in the Australian practice of 'shouting' drinks (if you have let the other members of a drinking group buy you drinks, you are obligated to 'shout' a round for the others in return — a clear instance of reciprocal obligation); participation in a democratic election (1973, pp. 47–9). Singer's reason for claiming that tacit consent need not be present in the two examples of quasi-consent seems to be his assumption that tacit consent must involve an 'inward' act of consenting, a 'saying in one's heart' that one consents, to be *actual* consent (1973, pp. 48–50). Obviously, I can let others shout drinks for me and can vote in an election without inwardly (or explicitly) consenting to buy drinks in return or inwardly consenting to be bound by the outcome of the election. What Singer calls 'quasi-consent' I am prepared to call 'tacit consent'

54

because I do not believe that a mental act of inwardly agreeing to do something is a necessary condition of tacit consent. Awareness that silence counts as tacit consent (rather than inwardly agreeing), combined with the other conditions of tacit consent (Chapter 2, see 'consent'), is sufficient for tacit consent. However, my main aim in commenting on Singer's notion of quasi-consent is not to show that letting others shout drinks for one or voting involves actual consent rather than quasi-consent, but to illustrate the point made in the text of the present book, viz. that the difference between Singer and myself on the present issue is only a terminological one. For we agree that, in the examples mentioned, voluntary acts create obligations; we only disagree whether the voluntary acts are properly called tacit consent or quasi-consent.

3. I here follow my 'In Defense of the Consent Theory of Political Obligation and Authority' (1977), in which I stressed that consent theory can be understood only if its precise and narrow characterisation of political obligation is appreciated. For a closely related and similarly narrow characterisation of political obligation see Simmons (1979, especially 11.11).

4. Why is secession to be allowed only for territorially concentrated groups? Normally, it is not practicable at present for two states to share legal sovereignty over the whole of their territory. Hence, if black Americans wanted to secede from the United States, this could not be accomplished by having two states with jurisdiction over the whole of the present territory of the United States and with two lots of citizens which are territorially intermingled.

5. This point is developed at much greater length by Dahl (1970) from a philosophical, and Ronen (1979) from an empirical, viewpoint. Dahl, arguing from liberal democratic principles, *advocates* that the present world order of about 150 sovereign states be replaced by an order in which there are more levels of authoritative political decision-making, i.e. an order in which there is genuine authoritative political power at the international, national and local community level. Ronen claims that *as a matter of fact* this change in the world order is already under way, i.e. that we have entered a period of disintegration into more and smaller 'socio-political' entitities and simultaneous integration into larger 'economic-normative' frameworks. Ronen claims that these two trends reinforce each other (p. 110).

6. I argue for this claim, in Chapter 6, in reply to John Kilkullen's objection to the reform version of consent theory.

7. The compatibility of individuality and sociability in modern liberal theory is one of the main themes of Gerald F. Gaus's book *The Modern Liberal Theory of Man* (1983).

8. For the distinction between individualist and collectivist versions of socialism see R.N. Berki (1975, p. 19) and Bhikhu Parekh (1975, pp. 4–5).

4

Consent and Three Versions of
Democratic Liberalism

Actual consent liberalism and its rivals

Most of the contemporary liberal democratic theorists who have
written on political obligation (in various senses of this term) deny
that consent is the basis of such an obligation. Within this literature
three approaches are most prominent. They are, very broadly
speaking, in the spirit of Locke, Kant and Hume respectively. Some,
most prominently Tussman, claim, in the spirit of Locke, that actual
personal consent is the basis of political obligation. The writers who
deny this divide into two camps. There are those, most prominently
Rawls, who, in the spirit of Kant, see as most important in justified
political obedience a natural duty to obey just states, and claim this
duty can be analysed in terms of hypothetical, rational, consent.
There are others, e.g. Steinberg, who, in the spirit of Hume, see
as most important in justified political obedience a natural duty to
obey states in so far as they have utility.

Since a theory of political obligation (in some sense of this term)
is a central part of a liberal democratic theory of the state, it may
be worthwhile to coin terms for these three versions of democratic
liberalism, viz. actual consent liberalism, hypothetical consent
liberalism and utilitarian liberalism.

Sometimes hypothetical consent and utilitarian liberal theorists
express their central objection to actual consent liberalism by
claiming that the ultimate criterion of political obligation is not
whether people have actually consented to a particular state but
whether the state in question is such that rational people ought,
morally speaking, to consent to it. If it is, then actual consent is,
at best, an unnecessary shuffle (Hume), at worst a normatively
improper shuffle (Steinberg) or an impossible shuffle (Rawls).

Using Rawls and Steinberg as the best contemporary examples of hypothetical consent and utilitarian liberalism respectively, I will show that their case against actual consent liberalism is unsound and that their approaches to justified political obedience are incomplete.

Hypothetical consent liberalism

John Rawls's *A Theory of Justice* (1971) is the best and the best-known example of hypothetical consent liberalism.[1] Rawls's main concern is to develop a theory of associational justice. But he also applies this theory to the issue of justified political obedience. Rawls distinguishes between natural duties and self-assumed obligations (1971, pp. 108–17). The latter refer to moral reasons for action which 'arise as a result of our voluntary acts' (1971, p. 113). Promissory obligation is a paradigm of self-assumed obligation. Natural duties are moral reasons for action which 'apply to us without regard to our voluntary acts' (1971, p. 114). As examples Rawls offers: the duty to help others when they are in need, the duty not to harm others and the duty not to inflict unnecessary suffering. Among natural duties is that of supporting and obeying just institutions, including just states. A just state, according to Rawls, is one whose rules and institutions are consistent with principles of justice which would be chosen by free and rational persons concerned to further their own interests in an initial position of equality and under a veil of ignorance regarding, *inter alia*, their status in society, their natural assets and abilities and their age, sex and special psychological propensities. Rawls claims that there are two principles of justice that would be chosen under these conditions.

First Principle. Each person is to have an equal right to the most extensive total system of basic liberties compatible with a similar system of liberty for all.

Second Principle. Social and economic inequalities are to be arranged so that they are both (a) to the greatest benefit of the least advantaged, and (b) attached to the offices and positions open to all under conditions of fair equality of opportunity (1971, p. 302).

According to Rawls, if a state is just, or nearly just, then we have a natural duty to obey it, regardless of whether we have actually consented to obey it. The duty to obey the state does not depend on *actual* consent but on it being a state consistent with the principles of justice chosen by hypothetical rational persons in the original position under a veil of ignorance.

Rawls grants that some persons also have an obligation to obey the state, i.e. a moral reason for obeying which is voluntarily assumed. But, he claims that:

> The natural duty of justice is the primary basis of our political ties to a constitutional regime . . . (and that) only the more favoured members of society (e.g. those who have chosen to assume political office) are likely to have a clear political obligation as opposed to a political duty (1971, p. 376).

Rawls does wonder whether the hypothetical parties in the original position would not make the requirement to comply with just institutions conditional on voluntary acts of individuals, e.g. on their having accepted the benefits of such institutions or their having undertaken to abide by them. He grants that the condition of such a voluntary act seems 'more in accordance with the contract idea with its emphasis upon free consent and the protection of liberty' (1971, p. 335). But he concludes that contractors in the original position would opt for an involuntary requirement of obedience to the state, since the first principle of justice already guarantees the full complement of equal liberties and since this is the easiest and most direct way to secure the stability of just institutions (1971, p. 336). Part of the problem, as Rawls sees it, of giving actual consent a more important role in a theory of justified political obedience, is that there does not seem to be any plausible candidate for a voluntary act that would create a (self-assumed) obligation to obey the state, since we are born into the state (1971, p. 337). At the beginning of his book Rawls already claims that no society can be a voluntary scheme in the literal sense since each person finds himself placed in some particular society at birth (1971, p. 13). In no more than three paragraphs of a very long book, consent-based political obligation, one of the most distinctive claims of democratic liberalism, is dismissed. (Cf. Pateman, 1979, p. 119.)

Rawls is correct in maintaining that there is a natural duty to obey just states (whether the Rawlsian analysis of natural duties is adequate need not be considered here). But it is a mistake to suppose his to be a sufficient account of justified political obedience, or that his case against actual, consent-based political obligation is sound. Rawls is, of course, also right that a more prominent place for consent-based political obligation than he admits is 'more in accordance with the contract idea with its emphasis upon free consent and the protection of liberty' (1971, p. 335). The question is whether he is right to make the following claims: first, that there is no suitable candidate for a voluntary act by virtually all citizens that could create a self-assumed political obligation; and, second, that, at any rate, the hypothetical contractors in the initial position would not make the natural duty of obeying just states dependent on any voluntary act.

Whether acceptance of membership in the state is a candidate for the voluntary act which creates political obligation Rawls does not consider. He takes it for granted that 'no society can be a scheme of co-operation which men enter voluntarily in a literal sense; each person finds himself placed at birth . . . in some particular society . . .' (1971, p. 13). But Locke recognised long ago that the issue here is not whether the citizenship of children (at birth!) could be voluntary. The issue is whether that of adults can be, given that they find themselves citizens of specific states when they cease to be political minors, and that there are no unoccupied territories to which dissenters could emigrate. Rawls does not consider this question, although he asserts, as he should within a consistent liberal democratic philsophy, that 'a society satisfying the principle of justice as fairness comes as close as a society can to being a voluntary scheme . . .' (1971, p. 13).

The following two legal rights would go a very long way towards making membership in the state voluntary for adults. First, the right of individuals to leave their states permanently and to change their nationality. Some of these individuals may move to other states which grant them entry. Others who wish to leave their states, but are not permitted entry by another state, may move to a dissenters' territory maintained outside the jurisdiction of all states. Second, the right of groups of individuals, who form the majority in the territory they occupy, to secede from their existing state.

There are no good reasons to suppose that states *cannot* grant their citizens such rights. Each right would of course be subject to conditions and qualifications, some of which are mentioned in Chapter 3 (as far as secession is concerned) and Chapter 6 (as far as emigration is concerned).

But these rights are not only possible: they follow from Rawls's first principle of justice, according to which '(e)ach person is to have an equal right to the most extensive total system of basic liberties compatible with a similar system of liberty for all'. For each citizen can have these rights without giving up any other basic liberties (or at least none as important as that of voluntary membership in the state) and the possession of these rights by any one citizen is quite compatible with all other citizens having the same rights.

This means that the following remarks of Rawls, already partly quoted, involve an imperfect appreciation of his own theory. He asks 'whether the parties in the original position would not do better if they made the requirement to comply with just institutions conditional upon certain voluntary acts . . .' He answers that 'nothing would be gained by this proviso' because the 'full complement of the equal liberties is already guaranteed' by the first principle of justice (1971, pp. 335–6). But Rawls overlooks that one of the liberties which the hypothetical contractors would choose under the first principle of justice is the right of emigration. For, the personal cost of not having such a right to a particular individual is potentially very high (if for cultural, professional, political, personal or other reasons he wishes to move to another state), while the cost to any particular individual of others having such a right is normally very small.

Hence Rawls would appear to be committed by his theory of justice (a) to the claim that membership in the state must be voluntary and, therefore, (b) to the further claim that obedience to a particular state is conditional on voluntary acceptance of membership in that state. And this voluntary acceptance of membership can generate a self-assumed obligation to obey the state.

The only claim made here is that voluntary acceptance of membership *can* generate a self-assumed obligation to obey the state, not that it *must*. For acceptance of membership which involves a mere thoughtless acquiescence in, rather than a knowing consent to, the requirements of membership, does not create a self-assumed obligation to comply. The consent which can generate political obligation is *needed* within a liberal democratic philosophy to provide a theoretical basis for political authority. (Rawls has not so far offered an account of the basis of political authority.) Hence, Chapter 7 proposes reforms ensuring that acceptance of membership in the state involves such consent as can generate political obligation and authority.

In short, Rawls is right to conclude that self-assumed obligations and natural duties are complementary, not mutually exclusive, grounds for obeying the state (1971, p. 337). But, as suggested, Rawls understates the complementary role of self-assumed obligations to obey the state. This is so because he overlooks the fact that he is committed to voluntary membership of the state by his hypothetical contractarianism, that such voluntary membership can be largely realised in practice and that, in an adequate liberal democratic theory of the state, an account of the natural duty to obey the state must be supplemented by an account of the basis of political authority and of that particular obligation to obey the state which is the correlative of it.

Utilitarian liberalism

The second alternative to actual consent liberalism is provided by utilitarian liberalism. To Locke's claim that the moral requirement to obey the state normally depends on the consent of the governed, David Hume's claim is opposed, this claim being that such a requirement rests directly on the utility of the state. The appeal to consent is therefore considered by Hume an unnecessary shuffle. In Rawls's version of democratic liberalism, consent (though not actual consent), does still play an essential part in justifying obedience to the state. For the nature of the just state, according to Rawls, can be explained only in terms of what hypothetical contractors would agree to in the original position. In utilitarian liberalism appeal to consent can be dispensed with altogether. Both utilitarian and hypothetical consent liberalism may say, by way of attack on actual consent liberalism that what matters regarding justified political obedience is not whether citizens have actually consented but whether it would be rational for them to consent. But this use of rational consent plays no essential role in utilitarian liberalism. Whereas in hypothetical consent liberalism, justice in the state is explained partly in terms of what it is rational to consent to, in utilitarian liberalism what it is rational to consent to is explained in terms of the utility of the state.

Jules Steinberg, in his book *Locke, Rousseau and the Idea of Consent* (1978), provides the fullest and clearest attack on actual consent liberalism from the viewpoint of utilitarian liberalism, as well as a sketch of the latter type of liberalism. Before proceeding, two terminological points require to be made. First, Steinberg calls his theory of political obligation teleological, not utilitarian. But one can treat his theory as utilitarian, since he defines a teleological theory of obligation as one which claims that obligations are determined by the consequences of actions. Second, Steinberg, unlike

Rawls, does not use different terms to refer to moral reasons for actions which arise out of our voluntary acts and those that do not. In what follows, therefore, obligation can refer to either type of reason.

Steinberg claims that appeal to consent as a basis of the obligation to obey the state is not merely an unnecessary shuffle, but one which 'is fundamentally incompatible with the normative logic characteristic of liberal democratic political thought' (1978, p. 9). Steinberg grants that the consent theory of political obligation is appealing to democratic liberalism: it appears to reconcile freedom with the need for law backed by sanctions. According to consent theory, the obligation to obey such laws rests on their voluntary acceptance by citizens. However, Steinberg argues that political obligation resting on consent is incompatible with two fundamental claims of democratic liberalism. The first claim is normative: whether a government ought, morally speaking, to be obeyed depends on the ends it pursues, not on whether one has agreed to obey it. The second claim is empirical: in a free society there is considerable moral disagreement and conflict of interests. This diversity of judgments among citizens means that the obligation to obey the law cannot rest on consent. For in a morally diverse and pluralistic society 'all citizens will not voluntarily agree to obey the same laws all the time' (1978, p. 104).

The non-consent version of democratic liberalism that Steinberg expounds acknowledges, none the less, the importance of personal freedom. It does so by advocating constitutional, limited government and by permitting maximum freedom in the private, i.e. non-governmental, sphere of life. The relationship between the citizen and the state, however, according to Steinberg, cannot be voluntary, for the state provides the coercive framework within which personal freedom becomes possible.

This is a stunted version of democratic liberalism, because it limits voluntary relations to the private sphere of life. The arguments for it rest on a misunderstanding of the place of consent in a liberal democratic philosophy and an underestimation of the extent of dissent which is compatible with a consent theory of political obligation.

Steinberg's normative objection to consent theory rests on a confusion. He assumes that consent to and utility of the state are alternative, mutually exclusive grounds of a moral obligation to obey the state. This assumption is mistaken. Democratic liberalism does indeed assert that we have a general natural obligation to obey the state in so far as it is necessary for the promotion of certain values, such as justice and human welfare. Consent has a place in liberal democratic theory, not as an alternative to the natural obligation grounded in the utility of the state, but as a complement to it, to explain how some specific citizens can have a moral right to govern others, given the assertion of some kind of equality among citizens. (In the present version of consent theory this assertion takes the form of an equal right of personal and, therefore, political self-determination.)

Steinberg's assumption that consent to and utility of the state are mutually exclusive grounds of political obligation rests on a failure to raise enough questions. He is right in indicating that we must ask whether states pursue the right ends. But we must also ask what gives particular individuals the moral right to occupy the seats of government, and this he fails to do. The mere fact that a group would pursue the right political ends if in office cannot give that group the moral right to occupy it, since there may be two groups which wish to occupy office, both of which would pursue the right ends equally effectively. Utility is most relevant to assessing whether a government is pursuing appropriate ends, consent to whether those who rule have a moral right to do so.

Steinberg's own teleological theory of justified political obedience is incomplete because he does not ask or answer the question as to what the basis of political authority is (what gives one the moral right to govern?). This omission, as well as his mistaken assumption that consent and utility are mutually exclusive considerations, is surprising, since he is aware that consent theorists introduce consent precisely to explain how some people can have a moral right to govern others (can have political authority), given that all people have equal moral rights (1978, p. 113, pp. 135–6). He comes close to indicating what he thinks the basis of political authority is, in the following response which he makes to the claim that democratic elections constitute a process of conferring authority. He asserts that 'it is not correct to say that the authority acquired by the winner of an election is a result of the consent of those freely participating in an election, since such *authority is actually conferred by law* and not consent' (1978, p. 120, author italics). But, at most, law confers a legal right to govern (authority legally speaking), not a moral right to do so (political authority). Hence, Steinberg offers no adequate alternative to consent as an account of the basis of political authority.

Steinberg claims that normatively liberal democratic theory has to rely on a telological, not a consent, approach. But he does nothing to develop such an approach to the issue of the basis of political authority. Nor do I know any systematic attempt in the literature to develop a utilitarian theory of the basis (as distinct from the justification) of political authority. Perhaps this is at least partly due to the failure of writers to distinguish between the justification and the basis of political authority. Flathman claims that his theory of political authority, developed at book length, is 'teleological in a somewhat hybrid . . . sense that might be abbreviated by calling it a utilitarianism of agency' (1980, p. 2). But he does not give any details of his version of utilitarianism and, therefore, cannot even attempt to relate it clearly to his theory of political authority. At any rate, Flathman's theory of political authority, though 'teleological in a somewhat hybrid sense', would not give Steinberg any comfort. This is so because Flathman claims that a necessary condition for a practice of political authority being justified is that it be compatible with the capacity for agency (i.e. 'for self-actuated, intentional and rational conduct') of the persons involved in the practice. Flathman, therefore, accepts the claim that 'political societies ought to be in some sense free or voluntary associations'. (1980, Part II, quotations from p. 177).

Well, is it possible to develop a utilitarian theory of political authority, which is consistent with liberal democratic principles but does not rely on consent as the basis of political authority? In trying to answer this question I will, for ease of exposition, assume one particular version of utilitarianism, viz. a version which is positive or maximising (as distinct from negative) and hedonistic. Two claims, already made above, will again be important. First, moral commonsense is right in holding that one can create a moral obligation and a moral right by promising. The presumption in favour of this claim should surely be overturned only by arguments stronger than any offered so far. Second, an adequate political philsophy cannot rest content with explaining how there can be a *legal* right to hold political office, but must explain a corresponding moral right or must, in some other way, go beyond merely legal issues to moral ones.

A version of rule-utilitarianism of the sort explained by Rawls in 'Two Concepts of Rules' (1955) is consistent with the claims just made. Such a version could assert that political authority is a practice which involves constitutive rules. Included in these is the rule that those who have political authority have a legal right to make decisions on behalf of those under authority and that the latter have a legal obligation to comply with these decisions. Obviously a hedonistic utilitarian claims that whether a practice of political authority should be adopted depends on whether adopting it would promote general happiness more than not doing so. Which alternative is the case would depend, *inter alia*, on the areas of life placed under the jurisdiction of political authority and on the criteria adopted for appointing persons to the office. (If only the senile were entitled to hold office and they had unlimited jurisdiction, then the practice would obviously not be justified!) So, rule-utilitarianism must answer two related but distinct questions regarding the practice of political authority: is it worth having in principle and, if there are a number of different possible practices, all of which are beneficial, which of these is most beneficial?

Now, presumably, a particular practice of political authority is morally justified if, and only if: (a) having a practice of political authority is more beneficial than not having it in principle; (b) the particular practice is more beneficial than any other practice that is possible at the time. Further, presumably, the legal right and obligation involved in a practice of political authority are supplemented by moral ones, if the practice does have a utilitarian justification. And one could add that the distinction between the justification and the basis of political authority can be made easily enough within this theory, and that, as already noted, whether a particular practice of political authority does have a rule-utilitarian justification depends in part on what is chosen as the basis of political authority, i.e. on what rule is adopted for appointing persons to political office.

It seems that, at least within a liberal democratic philosophy, this utilitarian theory of political authority is not acceptable. For it seems that, at least within such a philosophy, a utilitarian justification is neither necessary nor sufficient for the existence of political authority.

A utilitarian justification does not seem to be necessary for the existence of political authority. Assume that: (a) a practice of political authority — allowing some members to make some decisions for the community — has the support of the citizens of a state (perhaps it clearly has their consent: membership in the state is voluntary and governments are appointed by a method which has the citizens' consent); (b) this practice, while effective enough, does not maximise happiness; (c) the citizens know this but, nevertheless, prefer their practice of political authority to that which would maximise happiness. Surely, in this hypothetical case, we do have a government which has political authority[2], although the practice is not justified on utilitarian grounds: it does not maximise happiness.

The exercise of political power with a utilitarian justification does not seem to be sufficient for the existence of political authority either. Assume that, in the hypothetical community of the last paragraph, there are members of the armed forces who are committed utilitarians. Let them, by force, replace the existing political system by another the operation of which they rightly predict will maximise happiness. (Assume that the unhappiness caused by the coup and the short-term unpopularity of the new system is more than offset by the long-term increase in happiness due to the operation of the new system; the committed utilitarians rightly predict that the new political system will gain support within a decade or two.) Whatever non-democrats may say about the status of the utilitarian dictatorship, liberal democrats could hardly say that it is an authoritative government (has a moral right to hold office). In short, power exercised for the sake of maximising happiness, but against the wishes of the community, on liberal democratic principles at least, is political power but not political authority.

Thus, at least within a liberal democratic framework, utility is not an adequate alternative to consent for a theory of the basis of political authority. The utility of the state explains why, morally speaking, we ought to have it and why we will agree to have it, if we are rational. But it cannot in itself explain the authority of some specific persons to rule over others. That is explained through consent. Hence, the utility of and consent to the state are complementary and equally essential components of a complete liberal democratic theory of justified political obedience.

Steinberg's second claim, that consent cannot be a necessary condition of political obligation because of the moral pluralism of liberal democratic society, underestimates the extent of disapproval and dissent which is compatible with the consent theory of political obligation.

It is true that in a liberal democratic and, therefore, pluralist society there is no set of laws with which all citizens agree at any given time. However, citizens' consent does not require *agreement with*, in the sense of approval of, laws, but merely their *agreement to obey* laws, irrespective of whether they agree with them. Moreover, the agreement to obey law is wholistic, not selective. In accepting membership in a state one has to agree to comply with all the laws in existence (and future ones validly enacted). It is unrealistic to suppose that citizens can be given the opportunity to choose to agree to comply with some laws but not others. Of course, it does not follow from an agreement to obey law in general that one cannot be morally justified in breaking some particular law. For the agreement obligation to obey the law may be overriden by the moral wrongness of some law.

But why would anyone agree to obey the law in general knowing that there are, or probably soon will be, laws with which one disagrees or of which one even morally disapproves? Those who approve of the political system as such may agree to obey laws with which they disagree precisely because they know that unanimity on a set of laws is impossible. Some of these may agree to obey the law with every intention of honouring their agreement whether they approve of specific laws or not. Others may agree to obey the law in general, knowing that they consider themselves morally justified in breaking some laws on moral grounds, despite their agreement obligation to obey them. Some others, who disapprove of the political system as such, may yet agree to obey the law for various reasons. For example, some French communists may agree to obey French law rather than move to the Soviet Union because no true Frenchman would want to live anywhere but in France. Others may agree to obey the law because they wish to work for political change from within, legally or illegally.

Of those who agree to obey the law some may be legally released from the obligation to comply with one law or another by being granted the status of conscientious objector.

Those who do not wish to agree to obey the state should, according to liberal democratic principles, be permitted to emigrate or move to a dissenters' territory or, if they form a suitable group, to secede.

This may still leave some who refuse to obey the state in which they live but who are also unwilling or unable to leave it. A just liberal democratic state may be morally justified in expelling them or moving them to a dissenters' territory.[3]

The above remarks show that Steinberg is mistaken in claiming that the members of a pluralist society cannot be under consent-based political obligation.

It has not been my aim in this chapter to show that a hypothetical contract theory of associational justice is unsound; nor to show that the utility of the state is not a moral reason for supporting it. Rather it has been my aim to show that a liberal democratic theory of justified poltical obedience, whether developed along hypothetical contract or utilitarian lines, is incomplete if it does not give the actual consent of citizens to the state an adequate place. Actual consent cannot provide a complete theory of justified political obedience; it cannot, since the adoption of certain rules and aims by some individuals is, of course, not a sufficient condition for their being

just or worthwhile. The actual consent of citizens does not necessarily
make a state just or its ends worthwhile; but it provides the only
possible account within a liberal democratic theory of the basis of
political authority. Therefore, an adequate theory of justified political
obedience must refer to natural and to self-assumed obligations to
obey the state.

Notes

1. Hanna Pitkin also adopts this position in her widely read 'Obligation and Consent' (1965–6). See, as well, Russell Grice (1967, pp. 117–20).

2. Rousseau, of course, has denied this claim (*The Social Contract*, Book
III, Chapter XV). He is hardly a *liberal* democrat. But, more importantly,
his objections to representative democracy are unsound (see e.g. Plamenatz
(1967) Volume I, Chapter 10). Recently Pateman (1979) has repeated
Rousseau's case against representative democracy. I try later (Chapter 7,
see 'Political obligation and participatory democracy') to show that her
attack is unsound..

3. I claim only that such expulsion *may* be justified. Whether it is depends,
at least partly, on whether the persons involved not only refuse to agree
to obey the law but also actually break it and on whether it is possible for
individuals (as distinct from largish groups of people) to secede. (Compare
Chapter 3, 'Exposition', for a brief comment on the last issue.)

5

Three Versions of Actual
Consent Theory

The last two chapters try to make plausible the claim that an adequate theory of justified political obedience must offer an account
both of the substantive and the procedural reasons for obeying the
state. Substantive reasons account for the state as a worthwhile or
even necessary institution. They are to do with the justification of
political authority. Procedural reasons are concerned with the basis
of political authority, i.e. with what gives some particular individuals
the right to govern other particular individuals.

The last chapter depicts two versions of democratic liberalism
as alternatives to actual consent liberalism. These are shown to provide inadequate *alternatives* to a consent-based obligation to obey the
state. Instead, they must be recognised as offering possible reasons
for obeying the state (the natural obligation to obey states which
promote justice and human welfare) which *complement* the consent-
based obligation.

The membership version and its rivals

In Chapter 3 it is claimed that consent consists in acceptance of
full membership in the state. The present chapter considers two
alternative candidates for consent: participation in democratic elections of governments (the democracy version of consent theory) and
acceptance of the benefits of the law-abidingness of one's fellow
citizens (the reciprocal obligation version of consent theory). Neither
is an adequate candidate for the consent which is the basis of political
obligation and authority. But both still have a significant, if limited,
role to play in a theory of justified political obedience.

Before considering the two accounts of consent which are alter-

69

natives to the membership version of consent theory, it will be well to state clearly what such consent must be capable of explaining. Writers use the term 'political obligation' to refer to the obligation to obey the law or the state. Therefore, the content of political obligation can be identified as the obligation to comply with the constitution of the state, with all valid non-constitutional law and with constitutionally appointed governments. Also, political obligation is the correlative of political authority. Hence, the consent offered by consent theory must be a possible basis of political obligation and political authority and must be capable of accounting for all three components of political obligation.

The democracy version

Most of the few political philosophers who accept personal consent as the basis of political obligation and authority identify such consent with taking part in the democratic election of governments. D.D. Raphael (1970, Chapter IV), J. Plamenatz (1967, Volume 1, pp. 220–41), and R.S. Downie (1964, pp. 70-1) are three writers who accept the democracy version of consent theory.[1]

This version of consent theory asks us to assume that a group of people have to make a decision which is to be morally binding on all the members of the group and that unanimity among the group members as to which decision should be made is impossible within the time available. A voting procedure is a device which can solve such a problem since it is the known function of a voting procedure to achieve a decision which is morally binding on all participants in the procedure when unanimity is impossible. Therefore, any person who votes on an issue thereby puts himself under an obligation to abide by the outcome of the voting procedure. Someone who abstains from a vote on an issue may also be under an obligation to obey the outcome of the vote provided that certain conditions are fulfilled. The most important of these conditions is that he be under an obligation to use a voting procedure to decide the issue on which a vote is taken.

According to the democracy version of consent theory, this general model for creating obligations through a voting procedure has obvious application to democratic elections of governments. Government can be claimed to be a necessary means towards the promotion of justice and welfare. Unanimity among the members of the state on who should govern and with what policies is impossible.

But a voting procedure can be used to determine who shall govern and which political programmes should be adopted. The voters, in taking part in elections, put themselves under an obligation to obey the successful candidates and give these candidates the right to govern. So we have here a possible basis for the existence of an authority relation between a government and the governed. For, to take part in a voting procedure is to agree to the presupposition that the majority vote will be binding on all participants in the vote, whether they voted for or against the successful candidates. Those who abstain from the election are also under an obligation to accept the outcome, provided certain conditions are fulfilled. Of course, the theory continues, such a voting procedure only produces an outcome morally binding on the participants provided that there exist the liberties required to make the procedure fair and effective. These liberties include the freedom to stand as a candidate for political office, the freedom to form political parties which can campaign for candidates, and freedom of speech so that the merits of alternative candidates and policies can be argued publicly.

The democracy version of consent theory relies on a sound general model for creating a self-assumed obligation, that of a fair and effective voting procedure. Nevertheless, the democracy version has fatal flaws. These have nothing necessarily to do with the *de facto* shortcomings of elections, in other words with the various ways in which they are claimed by many writers to fall short of being fair and effective. (See, for example, Pateman, 1979, especially pp. 83–91, and Steinberg, 1978, Chapter 6.) For even if elections were so fair and effective that participation in them would create an obligation to accept the outcome, such participation would still not provide an adequate version of consent theory. Arguments (1) and (2) below show that voting in democratic elections is not necessary for political obligation and authority. Arguments (3) and (4) show that it is not sufficient.

(1) There are some members of democratic states who either do not have the legal right to vote in government elections or who do not have the opportunity to vote in a particular election. But it is not clear that the absence of this right or opportunity is sufficient for the absence of political obligation. For example, members of the British House of Lords do not have the legal right to vote in elections for seats in the House of Commons; the Governor-General of Australia does not have the legal right to vote in elections for the Lower or Upper House of the Australian Parliament. Are they

therefore not under political obligation? Citizens acquire the legal right to vote in elections at a certain age. Are those who reach this age between two elections not under political obligation until the next election? There are many people who do not have the opportunity to vote in a particular election, e.g. those who are too sick on the day. Are they therefore not under political obligation until the next election in which they do have such an opportunity? Admittedly, non-voters typically acquiesce in the outcome of elections. But if the democracy version were to claim that acquiesence without the right and opportunity to vote in the election is enough for the existence of consent, then it would be watering down consent to something which cannot generate an obligation or a right.

Perhaps this objection is not fatal to the democracy version, for it can respond in the way the membership version does in other contexts. (Chapter 6, see 'Objections from insufficient freedom of consent'.) That is, the democracy version can grant that at least some of the types of people mentioned in the objection are indeed not under political obligation and that the state in question does not have political authority over them. But it can add that this is not fatal to the democracy version; for the objection applies only to a small proportion of citizens. And, if the state in question is sufficiently just and welfare-promoting, then there will be a natural obligation to obey its law. Therefore, it does not follow from the lack of an authority relation between the state and the types of persons mentioned that they are morally free to break just and sensible laws. Hence no clearly unacceptable consequences follow from granting that the types of persons mentioned are not under political obligation.

Still, even if the present objection is not fatal to the democracy version, it remains that a version of consent theory which does not have the consequence of depriving a state of political authority over a citizen who happened (for example) to be too sick to vote in the last election would be preferable, *ceteris paribus*.

(2) It is possible to have a democratic state in which governments are not elected. John Burnheim proposes such a system in his article 'Statistical Democracy' (1981). Claiming that direct democracy is possible only in very small societies and noting some serious disadvantages of electoral representative democracy, he proposes a version of the ancient practice of selecting representatives on decision-making bodies by lot from those willing to serve on such bodies. The modern element is the proposal that sampling procedures be used in such a way that those selected to serve are numerically

proportionate to the different interest groups among those affected by the decisions of the decision-making body. If the members of a society adopt such a form of statistical democracy, it does not necessarily follow that they are not under political obligation. Yet they do not elect their governments. Moreover, the democracy version seems committed to the claim that the members of a state with a Burnheimian method of government selection can be under political obligation, viz. if such a method is adopted in a fair and effective referendum. The democracy version starts from the claim that the participants in a fair and effective voting procedure put themselves under an obligation to abide by the outcome of the vote. Hence, if the members of a society, adopt a Burnheimian form of government selection, in a fair and effective referendum, then they are under political obligation, through their participation in the referendum to obey resulting governments.

I have taken it for granted that Burnheim is correct in assuming that the method which he proposes for the selection of members of social decision-making bodies can be democratic. For present purposes, nothing hangs on this assumption. Whether or not states with governments selected by the Burnheimian method are democratic, it seems clear that such states can stand in a (consent-based) political authority relation to their citizens. Thus, participation in government elections is not necessary for political obligation or authority.

(3) What conditions must hold for an abstainer from a democratic election to be under an obligation to accept the outcome of the election? The mere fact that an election has taken place, that a given person had the legal right and the opportunity to take part in the election, and that he acquiesces in the outcome of the election, cannot create a promissory-type obligation on the part of the abstainer to accept the outcome of the election. It seems that the only thing which can create such an obligation on his part is a commitment by him, prior to the election, that the choice of government be made by a voting procedure. Therefore, the democracy version has to go outside its own terms if it is to explain the possible political obligation of election abstainers.

The same conclusion can be reached in the following way. Surely an election abstainer's acquiesence in the election outcome can only create an obligation to obey the government, if it can at all, provided that he is not coerced to be under the jurisdiction of the government from whose election he abstained. Raphael grants this. He writes that 'a citizen . . . who abstains, and who is prevented from

73

leaving the country, cannot be said to have accepted the government's authority or to be morally obliged' (1976, p. 113). In other words, the election abstainer can be under political obligation only provided that he has the legal right to leave the state, i.e. provided that, legally speaking, membership in the state is voluntary. But this means that the democracy version presupposes something, voluntary acceptance of membership in the state, which can provide an alternative account of the consent which creates political obligation, moreover an account not open to the present objections.

(4) The democracy version cannot explain all parts of political obligation. Political obligation includes both the obligation to obey the constitution — which contains the laws which specify how governments are to be selected — and the obligation to obey particular governments selected according to the constitution. Voting in an election can explain the obligation to obey the government which emerges from the election, but it cannot explain the obligation to obey the constitution. Of course, it may be suggested that in voting in an election one not only puts oneself under an obligation to obey the successful candidates, but also under an obligation to use the election procedure itself and to obey the whole constitution under which the election took place. However, there is a clear distinction between putting oneself under an obligation to do something by taking part in a vote to determine what should be done, and putting oneself under an obligation to use a voting procedure for determining issues of this kind on future occasions. Taking part in a vote to determine a result on a particular occasion does not in itself put one under an obligation to use this procedure in order to determine a result on future occasions. Hence to explain the political obligation to obey the constitution in general, and the democratic election procedure in particular (where it exists), one has to go beyond voting in democratic elections.

The above objections show that voting in democratic elections does not have sufficient scope to provide a general explanatory basis of political obligation and authority; it cannot explain political obligation and authority in all possible cases (objections 1, 2 and 3); nor can it explain all parts of political obligation (objection 4). Hence, for a sufficiently general basis of political obligation and authority, we must find something other than voting in democratic elections.

There is a possible variation on the democracy version of consent theory presented above which sidesteps the second of the four objections. Thus far it has been assumed that the democracy version claims that participating in democratic elections of representative governments is the only possible form consent could take. However, a contingent version of the theory would be more plausible. Such a version would still claim that, in liberal democracies, the consent which is the basis of political obligation and authority consists in voting in democratic elections. But it would not claim that this is the only form consent can take. The theory could grant that in other kinds of political systems political obligation and authority could be based on a consent which consists in some other action. One example of a version of consent theory which identifies consent with something other than participation in elections of representative governments may be Carole Pateman's theory of political obligation (1979). Following Rousseau she seems to identify consent with the participation of each citizen in the law-making of *direct* democracy.

It should be clear that both the contingent variation of the (representative) democracy version of consent theory in general, and Pateman's participatory democracy version of consent theory in particular, while side-stepping the second of the above objections, are still subject to the first and, more importantly, the third and fourth of the objections.

Consent as acceptance of membership in the state does provide a sufficiently general basis of political obligation and authority. It can account for the political obligation to obey the constitution, including the rules for holding elections (if this is the method of selecting governments), as well as the obligation to obey governments that emerge from particular elections. It can account for the political obligation to obey democratically elected governments and for the obligation to obey governments created by non-elective democratic procedures. It can account for the political obligation of those too sick to vote in a particular election, for in accepting membership in the state they have agreed to obey constitutionally created governments, even if due to misadventure they cannot take part in an election. And it can account for the political obligation of election abstainers, for in accepting membership in a state in which governments are democratically elected, they have put themselves under an obligation to accept the outcome of legally conducted elections, even if they abstain from them. Hence voting in democratic elections does not, while accepting membership in the state does, provide a form of consent which has the scope for an adequate theory of political obligation and authority.

However, it has also been shown that voting in a fair and effective election puts the voters under an obligation to accept the outcome of the election. Thus it is equally proper to conclude that, in those states in which governments are returned in fair and effective democratic elections, voting in such elections puts the voters under an obligation to obey the government that is elected and gives such a government a right to the obedience of those who voted in the election. The obligation of the voters to obey and the right of the government to obedience is distinct from, and additional to, any other obligation to obey and any other right to obedience which voters and government respectively may have, e.g. distinct from, and additional to, the political obligation and authority created by acceptance of membership in the state.

Voting in fair and effective elections puts voters under an obligation to comply with the government that is elected. There is no need to reply to moral or empirical objections to the effect that elections in existing states are not sufficiently fair or effective. For this book only claims that those who vote in elections put themselves under an obligation to comply with the resulting governments *if* these elections are fair and effective. But replies need to be given to two often stated logical objections. (See, for example, Pateman, 1979, pp. 87–8.) It is sometimes objected that revolutionaries who vote for a revolutionary party do not mean to obligate themselves to comply with the result of the election. Such revolutionaries, it is said, wish to overthrow the existing political system, use liberal democratic elections only to publicise their cause and may have little intention to comply with the government that results from the election. This objection wrongly assumes that a promise-like act fails to come off if the person performing the act does not intend to be bound by it. But, just as a deceptive promise is still a promise and creates a promissory obligation, so those who vote in an election are obligated to accept the outcome whether they intend to obligate themselves by voting or not. This is so because it is the generally known function of a voting procedure to produce an outcome which is binding on those who take part in the vote. A second objection sometimes made is that a Nazi-like, i.e. an evil, political party may win an election and be legally entitled to govern. Surely, it is objected, those who voted against this party are not morally obligated to comply with it. This objection overlooks the fact that the consent-based moral obligation to comply with the evil government would be overridden by other moral considerations if this government did enact evil laws.

In those states where fair and effective elections are held, voting creates obligations and rights additional to those created by accepting membership in the state. But it is not enough merely to acknowledge such voting as an additional source of obligations and rights. Rather it has to be stressed that, if people have a right to personal self-determination, then not only must membership in the state be voluntary, but members *must* have the right to participate in political decision-making. Circumstances can perhaps be imagined in which such self-determining persons may temporarily not exercise this right and temporarily adopt a non-democratic method for selecting governments (e.g. in times of war). But under normal circumstances, only a democratic procedure for making political decisions is compatible with the liberal democratic assumptions about human nature. Such procedures could take the form of participatory or representative democracy. In both cases, most citizens will put themselves under an obligation to obey the law additional to that created by acceptance of membership in the state. For most, in a politically healthy state, will either take part in voting to create laws directly or in voting to appoint representatives whose duty it is to create laws. (Burnheim's proposal (1981), already mentioned, for a non-elective form of representative democracy, is left aside here, since it needs further development to assess whether statistical democracy is preferable to elective democracy and since all existing representative democracies are elective ones.)

In short, given liberal democratic assumptions about human nature, the liberal democratic state must provide for two kinds of consent: that involved in acceptance of membership in the state and that involved in creating law directly or *via* representatives by means of voting procedures.

The reciprocal obligation version

A number of writers are attracted by the idea that, at least within a liberal democratic philosophy, political obligation must rest on a voluntary act. Finding the membership version of consent theory implausible, they have suggested that the act in question may be the voluntary acceptance of the benefits of the law-abidingness of one's fellow citizens. Among such writers are Hart (1955, especially pp. 185–6), Rawls (1964), Jeffrie G. Murphy (1971, especially pp. 66–7) and David A.J. Richards (1971, especially p. 155). (Rawls, however, had abandoned the present theory by the time he wrote

A Theory of Justice. See Simmons (1979, pp. 143–6).) The following account of political obligation as reciprocal obligation is developed from the accounts given by the writers mentioned but is not meant to be identical with that of any one of them.

If I freely accept a good deed from you, then I have an obligation to return a good deed to you if the need for it arises. For example, if you lend me some money when I badly need it, then in accepting the loan I put myself under an obligation to help you in an appropriate way should you get into difficulty. Let us call this an obligation of reciprocation.

Now assume that a number of persons undertake a joint enterprise within the framework of a rule-governed association; that, if the aims of the association are achieved, the members of the association are better off than they would be without this association, *mutatis mutandis*; and that the association could not achieve its objectives unless most of its members obeyed most of its rules most of the time.

The state can be seen as such an association, that is, as a joint enterprise of a great number of persons conducted within the framework of associational rules, namely law. At least according to liberal democratic theory, if the proper aims of the state are achieved, then its members are better off than they would be without the state, *mutatis mutandis*; and it is unlikely that the state could achieve its aims unless most people did obey most laws most of the time. Hence any citizen who accepts the benefits of the law-observance of others has an obligation to observe the law himself so that others may have the benefit of his law-observance.

So we have here identified a voluntary act, one's acceptance of the benefits of the law-observance of others, which creates a moral obligation to observe the law oneself — an obligation of reciprocation. Since this obligation is one to observe the law, it is entirely appropriate to call it political obligation.

Two further points need to be made in even a brief exposition of the theory of political obligation seen as reciprocal obligation. First, the obligation in question is clearly one that one owes to one's fellow citizens. For an obligation to return a benefit is an obligation to the person from whom one has received a benefit. Second, the proportion of citizens who have such an obligation to reciprocate will be the greater, the more just is the state in which they live. Consider a case where all citizens of a state are better off than they would be without it, *mutatis mutandis*, but where a minority of citizens receive a grossly unfair proportion of the benefits of having the state. This minority benefits so much from the law-observance of their less fortunate fellow citizens that they are presumably under an obligation of reciprocation despite the injustice of their state; but it is far more open to doubt whether the exploited majority are under such an obligation. So in order to make it most plausible that virtually all citizens are under political obligation, understood as an instance of reciprocal obligation, it is best to specify that this obligation is conditional on a state being reasonably just.

Though the voluntary acceptance of the benefits of the law-observance of others can create an obligation to observe the law, this acceptance is not an act on which a sound theory of political obligation and authority can be built. Four objections may be raised:

(1) The reciprocal theory of political obligation seems too narrow since it cannot account for the political obligation we may have to obey paternalistic laws.[2] Laws which prohibit harming others may be called other-directed laws and those which prohibit self-inflicted harm may be called self-directed, or paternalistic, laws. Obvious examples of the former category are laws against killing and injuring others and laws against theft. A plausible example of paternalistic law is that requiring the wearing of car seat-belts.

This is a plausible rather than obvious example since one can think of non-paternalistic reasons for the legal requirement to wear car seat-belts: wearing them reduces the rate of serious injuries in accidents and, therefore, the cost to the community of medical treatment and invalid pensions. However, the non-paternalistic reasons for the legal compulsion to wear car seat-belts could be largely removed by other policies. If cars were legally required to carry seat-belts, adequate publicity given to the benefits of wearing them, and drivers who refused were required to pay higher insurance premiums, then the proportion of motorists who did not wear them would probably be small. Then the reduction in the rate of injuries consequent on a legal compulsion to wear car seat-belts would probably be so small that the increase in general insurance premiums required to pay for them, if there were no such legislation, would be too small to count as harm to others. But *ex hypothesi* a small proportion of drivers might still refuse to wear seat-belts unless this was legally required. And some people might then still argue for such legal compulsion *on paternalistic grounds*.

Putting the point more generally: there is probably no conduct that might be banned by paternalistically motivated legislation which does not have *effects* on others as well as the actors themselves. But we can distinguish between effects (even negative effects) on others and harming others. Not every minor negative effect that one's actions have on others actually harms them. (Farting in public offends, but it does not harm.) Given the distinction between other-regarding and self-regarding legislation in terms of *harming*, not in terms of affecting others, some of the legislation that is usually regarded as paternalistic legislation will be so according to the rough characteristisation given above. (For a list of putatively paternalistic legislation see Gerald Dworkin, 1971.)

Now to return to the claim that the reciprocal theory of political obligation cannot account for the political obligation we may have to obey paternalistic legislation. If my fellow citizens obey other-directed laws, I certainly benefit in not being killed, injured or deprived of my possessions; and very plausibly I have an obligation to them to reciprocate by obeying these laws myself so that they have the corresponding benefit of my law-observance. But this model of reciprocal obligation completely fails to fit the obligation to obey paternalistic laws. I do not benefit from the observance of such laws by others; hence, I cannot have an obligation of *reciprocation to others* to follow such laws myself. And even if I did have an obligation of reciprocation to obey paternalistic laws, my observance of such laws could not count as fulfilling this obligation. For to fulfil an obligation of reciprocation is to return a benefit for a benefit received. But since my observance of a paternalistic law does not benefit others, such observance of mine cannot count as fulfilling such an obligation.

(2) The reciprocal theory of political obligation also cannot account for the political obligation which we may have to observe laws which prohibit harming one's own (or stray or wild) animals. Again the model of reciprocal obligation seems quite inappropriate. I do not benefit from you harming your dog and you do not benefit from my not harming my dog. Hence I cannot have an obligation of *reciprocation to you* not to harm my dog; and, at any rate, my not harming my dog cannot count as fulfilling a reciprocal obligation to you.

It may be suggested in reply to objections (1) and (2) that the reciprocal obligation principle should be applied to the system of law as a whole only, not to particular types of law, e.g. paternalistic laws. That is to say, it may be suggested that the reciprocal obligation to obey the law applies on a wholistic rather than on a selective basis: if I benefit from the observance by others of *the whole body of law*, then I have an obligation of reciprocation to obey *the whole body of law* myself so that others can benefit from my law-observance.

This reply to objections (1) and (2) points to a feature of political obligation which is worth noting. Let us ask: is political obligation wholistic or selective with regard to (valid) laws? That is to say: if I am under political obligtion, am I under an obligation to observe *all* the laws of the state or is it possible to have an obligation to obey only *some* of the laws of the state? It seems it must be the former. What a government has authority to do is determined by the constitution. Hence, if the legislation a government enacts is valid then the government is acting within its authority. But since political authority and political obligation are correlatives, any law the government has authority to enact the citizens must be under political obligation to obey. Hence political obligation is wholistic rather than selective with respect to law; if one is under political obligation then one is under an obligation to obey all the laws in existence.

The membership version of consent theory is consistent with and explains the wholistic nature of political obligation. In accepting membership of the state one puts oneself under the authority of the (constitutional) government of the state and agrees to obey *all* the laws of the state; members of associations cannot pick and choose among the rules of the association: if they want membership they must agree to obey all the rules of the association.

However, on the reciprocal obligation account of political obligation there does *not* seem to be any reason why political obligation should be wholistic. On the contrary: if the basis of my political obligation is the benefits I have received through the law-observance of others, then my obligation to obey extends only to those laws from whose observance I have benefited and whose observance by me will benefit others.

To expand the point, we may say that the whole body of law consists, *inter alia*, of laws whose observance:

(a) prevent harm to other persons;
(b) prevents harm to oneself;
(c) prevents harm to animals.

Since my fellow citizens do not receive any extra benefits if I observe laws of type (b) and (c), it is quite unclear why observance of paternalistic and animal welfare laws should be required by the reciprocal obligation account of political obligation.

(3) Consent theory claims that natural obligations to obey the state cannot explain the existence of an authority relation between the state and its citizens and that, for this reason, a voluntary act has to be introduced into an adequate liberal democratic theory of

justified political obedience. Hence the voluntary act which explains political obligation must also explain its correlative, political authority. But the voluntary act which creates the reciprocal obligation to obey the law is not such an act. Accepting the law-abidingness of one's fellow citizens can create a reciprocal obligation to comply with the law but not the political authority of governments.

(4) To succeed at all, the reciprocal obligation version of consent theory must virtually fall back on the membership version at a crucial point. Supporters of the reciprocal obligation version tend to claim that acceptance of the benefits of the law-observance of one's fellow citizens has to be a 'voluntary act' in order to create a reciprocal obligation to obey the law (see Rawls, 1964, and Richards, 1971). At any rate it is clear that, if one is coerced to accept benefits one does not wish to accept, then no obligation to reciprocate is created. Hence the reciprocal obligation account of political obligation, to be acceptable, must specify that persons who are claimed to have such obligations are not coerced to accept the benefits in question or deliberately prevented from avoiding the acceptance of these benefits. But to specify this is to make membership in the state voluntary. For if some citizens (or the government) prevent others from leaving the state then they are deliberately depriving them of the opportunity to avoid accepting benefits (the law-observance of their fellow citizens) which they do not wish to accept. Hence the reciprocal obligation version presupposes something — uncoerced acceptance of membership in the state — which is itself a possible basis for an alternative account of political obligation not open to the present objections to the reciprocal obligation version of consent theory.

The voluntary acceptance of the benefits of the law-observance of one's fellow citizens is not an act on which an adequate theory of political obligation can be built. This is so, since it cannot account for the possible political obligation to obey paternalistic laws or laws protecting the welfare of animals, since it cannot provide a basis of political authority, and since it presupposes voluntary acceptance of membership in the state — the very act to which it is meant to be a preferable alternative. Moreover, the membership version of consent theory can account for the obligation to obey paternalistic and animal welfare laws and can provide an adequate basis for political authority.

But just as the democracy version of consent theory points to an important additional source of self-assumed obligation to obey the state, so does the reciprocal obligation version. To the extent that citizens voluntarily accept the benefits of the law-observance of others, subject to the justice condition already mentioned, to that extent do they assume a reciprocal obligation to obey the law. And in any just state, most citizens would indeed receive such benefits.

The result of the discussion in Chapters 3 to 5 of possible sources of an obligation to obey the state is as follows. Consent theory uses 'political obligation' to refer to one particular obligation to obey the state. This is the obligation which is the correlative of political authority. Its existence is only a reason (an exclusionary, but not an indefeasible, reason) for obeying the state. I refer to this feature of political obligation as the narrow scope of consent theory. The obligation to which it gives rise is to obey the constitution, constitutionally enacted laws and constitutionally appointed governments. The obligation is 'wholistic', requiring compliance with *all* the laws that apply to a particular person. Therefore, neither consent as voting in government elections, nor as acceptance of the benefits of the law-abidingness of one's fellow citizens, has sufficient scope to explain the whole of political obligation. The former cannot explain the obligation to comply with the constitution. The latter cannot explain the obligation to comply with paternalistic or animal welfare legislation. The consent which creates political obligation and authority has to consist in accepting membership in the state, because only such consent can explain the whole of political obligation and provide a basis for political authority and ensure that the citizen is a voluntary member rather than a captive of the state.

In so far as a state is successful in promoting liberty, justice and welfare, there is also a general natural obligation to obey it. Those who vote in particular elections put themselves under a further self-assumed obligation to obey governments created in such elections, whether they voted for or against the successful candidates. And in the reasonably just kind of state we are envisaging, the vast majority of citizens would also be under a self-assumed reciprocal obligation to obey other-regarding laws.

There is one further self-assumed obligation to comply with the law which must be mentioned since it will be found in at least every reasonably just state. As Rawls notes (1971, p. 344), those who voluntarily assume an official position within the state apparatus (whether legislative, executive, judicial, military or civil service) put themselves under a self-assumed obligation to comply with the law which is distinct from and additional to all the other obligations mentioned.

Notes

1. A. Gewirth (1962) and S.I. Benn and R.S. Peters (1969, especially pp. 326–31 and 343–4) also link political obligation and authority with voting in democratic elections but less closely so than do Raphael, Plamenatz and Downie. Nevertheless, the third and fourth objections made below to the theory as held by the latter writers also apply to the version of the theory held by Gewirth and Benn and Peters.

2. Neither Hart nor Rawls nor Richards is likely to claim that paternalistic laws should not be enacted by the state. Hart's remarks in *Law, Liberty and Morality* (1969), pp. 30-4, make it fairly clear that he is in favour of some paternalistic legislation. Rawls's hypothetical contractors in the original position would, presumably, agree on a principle requiring paternalism. For they would know that some adults do extremely harmful, irreversible acts which they later regret having done. And they would agree that they would like to be stopped by others should they ever want to do such irrational acts themselves. Compare Richards (1971, p. 192).

6

Replies to Objections

Defence of a reform version of consent theory assumes that existing liberal democratic governments may lack political authority. This assumption some writers regard as repugnant to common sense. For example Hanna Pitkin in her 'Obligation and Consent, I' (1965), wrote that:

> . . . consent theory is much troubled by the difficulty of showing that you, or a majority of your fellow-citizens . . . have in fact consented . . . Of course, these facts need not invalidate the consent argument. Perhaps most of us are not really obligated in modern, apathetic mass society; perhaps our government is not really legitimate. But such conclusions seem to fly in the face of commonsense. Surely, one feels, if the present government of the United States is not a legitimate authority, no government has ever been (1965, p. 994).

The hypothetical claim of Pitkins's last sentence seems to be of the 'if-this-is-not-true-I'm-a-Dutchman' kind, i.e. it appears to assert as obvious that the 1965 United States Government possessed legitimate authority.

Radical political philosophers, such as Marxists and anarchists, have never thought the denial of the claim to legitimate authority of liberal democracies contrary to commonsense. Some conservative and liberal political philosophers also deny that contemporary liberal democratic states have political authority (see Michael Oakeshott 1975, pp. 191–3, H. Arendt 1954, and Simmons 1979). In a 1972 reprinting of her 1965 article (in *Philosophy, Politics and Society*, Fourth Series) Pitkin, too, distanced herself from the claim that such denial lacks common sense.

The question whether the governments of liberal democracies have political authority can, therefore, be regarded as an open one; one which cannot be answered without an adequate theory of political authority.

This book defends a reform, not a *status quo*, version of consent theory. The kind of objections it deals with are those which attempt to show, not just that, as a matter of fact, consent-based political obligation does not exist for most citizens, but that it is unnecessary, undesirable or impossible. The objections dealt with are restricted to those which can be made from within the liberal democratic tradition (taking 'liberal' in the broadest possible sense). Objections which depend on assumptions or claims made within the radical or conservative traditions of political philosophy are not discussed. First, the aim of the book is to show that consent must have a place within a liberal democratic philosophy which is denied to it by most liberal democratic theorists. Second, to assess the merits of the liberal democratic tradition as compared to the radical and conservative traditions would require a book of its own. Apart from this restriction, the discussion of objections is more comprehensive than heretofore, taking account of the paucity of written replies to the many objections to consent theory found in the literature.[1]

On Wolff crying anarchism

One objection to consent theory arises out of R.P. Wolff's notorious argument for what he calls 'philosophical anarchism' (1970).[2] Though this argument has attracted much criticism, it appears that Wolff still considers it basically sound, as does K. Graham. (For criticism of Wolff, see Bates, 1972, Smith, 1973 and Pritchard, 1973, among others; for Wolff's replies see Wolff, 1973; for the one piece in support of Wolff's argument, see Graham, 1982).

According to Wolff, the basic question of political philosophy is this: how can the moral autonomy of the individual be made compatible with the legitimate authority of the state?

By moral autonomy, Wolff means acceptance of final responsibility for deciding what one ought to do, morally speaking. By legitimate authority he means the moral right to rule.[3] From this basis Wolff argues thus for anarchism:

The defining mark of the state is authority, the right to rule. The primary obligation of man is autonomy, the refusal to

86

be ruled. It would seem, then, that there can be no resolution of the conflict between autonomy of the individual and the putative authority of the state. (1970, p. 18.)

For if the individual retains his autonomy by reserving to himself in each instance the final decision whether to co-operate, he thereby denies the authority of the state; if on the other hand, he submits to the state and accepts its claim to authority, then . . . he loses his autonomy. (1970, p. 40.)

If authority and autonomy are genuinely incompatible only two courses are open to us. Either we must embrace philosophical anarchism and treat *all* governments as non-legitimate bodies whose commands must be judged and evaluated in each instance before they are obeyed; or else we must give up as quixotic the pursuit of autonomy in the political realm and submit ourselves . . . to whatever form of government appears most just and beneficent at the moment. (1970, p. 72.)

It is out of the question to give up the commitment to moral autonomy (1970, pp. 71–2). There would appear to be no alterntive but to embrace the doctrine of anarchism and categorically deny *any* claim to legitimate authority by one man over another. (1970, p. 72.)

These quotes slightly oversimply Wolff's position. He grants there is one way in which political authority and moral autonomy can be made compatible, viz. through unanimous direct democracy. If it is a necessary condition of the validity of a law that all members of the polity vote for it then the citizens would only be obeying themselves in obeying the government which enforces such a law. However, this proposal 'is so restricted in its application that it offers no serious hope of ever being embodied in an actual state' (1970, p. 69).

Wolff has made two different claims about legitimate authority: that it is impossible and that it is undesirable. In 'On Violence' (1969) Wolff claimed that 'the notion of legitimate authority . . . is . . . inherently incoherent' (p. 602). But Wolff's *In Defense of Anarchism* (1970) no longer contends that (legitimate) political authority is logically impossible; but rather that the state which has (legitimate) authority either has to be a unanimous direct democracy (an

87

unrealistic alternative) or has to have members who have given up moral autonomy (a price which one could, but ought not to, pay for (legitimate) authority).

Let us turn to the second of these claims, viz. that authority is undesirable. Central to it is the incompatibility thesis (IT): the claim that in any state, other than unanimous direct democracy, there must be a logical conflict between citizens' obligation of personal autonomy and the state's political authority. It may help to say at the outset what is wrong with Wolff's argument for IT: he seems to assume that the reason for action created by the command of someone in authority is one which cannot be overridden by any other reason. But such a command is only a defeasible reason (though an exclusionary one) for action, not an indefeasible reason.

According to the analysis of authority-over developed in Chapter 2, if Chief has authority over Indian with respect to a specified sphere of action, then Chief's command to Indian to do X is a reason for Indian to do X. This reason is exclusionary, but not indefeasible. This account seems adequately to capture our pre-theoretical beliefs regarding the force of a command (the demand of someone in authority). Unlike the demands of those who have no authority over Indian, such demands carry *some* weight in themselves (i.e. apart from the merit of doing the action as such); moreover, such demands seem to make it appropriate to disregard some reasons for action, such as the inconvenience of doing it when commanded or somewhat greater good resulting from doing an action other than that commanded.[4] Yet one *can* be morally justified in disobeying commands; hence the reason for action created by a command is not indefeasible. A command does not exclude all moral reasons for counting against it and some of these moral reasons can outweigh the command.

In the political sphere these commonsense beliefs about the force of the commands of political authority are reflected in the framework within which morally justified civil disobedience is usually discussed. It is generally agreed that civil disobedience can be morally justified in a state which has political authority and by persons who are under political obligation. To claim that civil disobedience of government, unlike rebellion against a government, is morally justified, is not to deny that the government has authority to govern. It is only to claim that there are moral considerations which override the government's right to require certain actions from its citizens.

If the above analysis of an authority-over relationship in terms of reasons for action is correct, then political authority and moral autonomy are not logically incompatible. In Wolff's terms, this claim can be put as follows. If I am a morally autonomous person, the government's 'commands must be judged and evaluated in each instance before they are obeyed' (1970, p. 71). That this is true does not mean that the government has no right to require me to act in certain ways. It has such a right even if I decide not to obey the command. Wolff is mistaken in claiming that, 'if the individual retains his autonomy by reserving to himself in each instance the final decision whether to co-operate, he thereby denies the authority of the state' (1970, p. 40).

Wolff's IT would be correct only if the reason for action created by a command of political authority either excluded or outweighed all possible reasons against doing the commanded action. If this were so there would be no reason that could defeat the reason created by the command. Consequently one could not be morally justified in disobeying a command of a government which has political authority over one; hence there could be no logical room for exercising moral autonomy.

Wolff gives no argument for the view that the determinations of political authorities create reasons for action which exclude or outweigh all other possible reasons for action. No good argument for such a view is available. But there is an appearance of such an argument in Wolff's *In Defense of Anarchism*, at those points where the author explores what it is to obey a command. Consider the following passages from Wolff's book:

> When I am commanded to do something, I may chose to comply even though I'm not being threatened, because I am brought to believe that it is something which I ought to do. If that is the case, then I'm not, strictly speaking, obeying a command, but rather acknowledging the force of an argument or the rightness of a prescription. (1970, p. 6.)

> Obedience is not a matter of doing what someone tells you to do. It is a matter of doing what he tells you to do *because he tells you to do it*. (1970, p. 9.)

> Taking responsibility for one's actions means making the final decisions about what one should do. For the autonomous man, there is no such thing, strictly speaking, as a *command*. (1970, p. 15.)

[In so far as a man is autonomous] he will resist the state's claim to have authority over him. That is to say he will deny that he has a duty to obey the laws of the state *simply because they are the laws.* (1970, p. 18.)

From these passages one might fairly derive this argument:

(1) If one is obeying authority, one is obeying the commands of authority.

(2) If one is obeying a command to do X, one is doing X *simply* because it is commanded. (The argument for this second premise would be that one cannot both be obeying a command to do X and acknowledging the force of an argument to do X.)

(3) If one is doing X *simply* because it is commanded, one is not acting autonomously.

Therefore, (4) If one is obeying authority, one is not acting autonomously.

Premise (2) and the argument for it are equally dubious. If this premise is true, then it is logically impossible to obey a command to do X which one believes to be justified since one thinks X does indeed need doing. According to Wolff: if manager M orders subordinate S to do X, and S asks why he should do X, then only if M fails to give S good reasons and S cannot think of any himself for doing X, is S in a position to obey the command 'strictly speaking. Indeed such a request for reasons would be an act of insubordination since it shows that S does not wish to obey the command 'strictly speaking'.

On the face of it, it seems correct to distinguish between two kinds of obeying of a command to do X: (a) obeying it simply because one has been ordered to do X and (b) obeying it partly because one thinks there are good reasons for doing X independently of the command. Surely, this is a distinction *within* obeyed commands not only in ordinary language but also 'strictly speaking'. After all, the enlightened manager who advises his staff not to obey his orders without understanding the reasons for doing the required actions, cannot plausibly be held to be contradicting himself. In short, the distinction between blind obedience and thinking (or rational or considered) obedience is one between two kinds of obedience, not between obedience and something else.

It is possible that conflict may arise between moral autonomy and political authority (between what the citizen decides he morally ought to do and what his state has a right to have him do). But the fact of such conflict would not show that what seemed to be the state's right was not. Wolff may well be correct in claiming that there cannot be a form of government (other than a direct democracy of an unrealistically unanimous kind) which would make it impossible for a conflict to arise between political obligation and other moral considerations. But the presence of such conflict does not show that a government cannot have political authority over morally autonomous persons.

Objections which misunderstand the scope of consent theory

Two often stated objections lose their plausibility once the precise and narrow scope of consent theory is understood. H.A. Prichard (1968, Chapter 4), Margaret MacDonald (1963), T.D. Weldon (1953), J.C. Rees (1954), and Thomas MacPherson (1967) all claim that classical political philosophy rests on a mistake. Their argument for this claim runs roughly thus. The problem of political obligation — Why should I or anyone obey the state? — is the fundamental problem of political philosophy. Classical political philosophy assumes that there is a single answer to this question; for example, that the state has the consent of its members or that it promotes the general good. But there is no single answer to this question, for the reasons why one should obey (or disobey) the law depend on the circumstances of particular cases. Deeply committed democrats may (rightly) think they ought to obey a dictator if this is the least evil possible under certain circumstances; and they may (also rightly) think they are not morally required to obey a genuinely democratic government which refuses, for no sufficient reasons, to let them leave the country. As MacDonald puts it, 'there is no general criterion' of political obligation (no 'sole justification for accepting any or every law'), 'but an indefinite set of vaguely shifting criteria, differing for different times and circumstances . . . '. She adds: '(n)o general criterion of all right actions can be supplied. Similarly, the answer to 'Why should I obey *any* law, acknowledge the authority of *any* State or support *any* Government?' is that this is a senseless question' (1963, pp. 183–5).

As a criticism of consent theory this objection is misconceived. For consent theory claims only that the particular obligation to obey the state which is the correlative of political authority must be based on consent, not that any obligation whatsoever must be so based. In other words, consent theory claims (at least within liberal

democratic theory) that consent must be used to distinguish between
governments which have political authority and those which do not;
but it does not propose to answer the question 'Why should I obey
any law . . . or support *any* government?' solely in terms of consent.
Consent theory is quite consistent with MacDonald's claim that the
answer to the last question cannot be given in terms of necessary
and sufficient conditions, without, however, being committed to this
claim.

The plausibility of Hume's frequently repeated objection to
consent as an 'unnecessary shuffle' (Hume, 1964, compare Quinton,
1968, p. 12 and MacCormick, 1979, p. 403) also depends on a failure
to recognise the precise scope of consent theory.[5] Steinberg's variation on Hume's objection (in which the 'shuffle' becomes a normatively improper one) was dealt with earlier (see Chapter 4). Hume
may be interpreted to claim less than Steinberg, namely that the
'shuffle' is unnecessary, but not necessarily improper. Consequently,
Hume's own version may be thought to be less vulnerable. I propose to show that it is no less vulnerable.

After presenting a number of objections to contract and consent
theory, Hume develops the following 'more philosophical refutation
of this principle of an original contract or popular consent' in his
'Of the Original Contract' (1964, p. 366). He distinguishes between
two sorts of duties: those which we perform from such natural
inclination as love of children, gratitude and pity, and those which
we perform, not from such natural inclinations, but from a sense
of obligation, from the consideration that society is impossible if
they are not performed. An example of the former type of duty is
the duty parents have to provide for their offspring; an example of
latter is the duty of fidelity, i.e. of keeping one's promises. Hume
asserts that the political duty of allegiance is of the second type where
inclination is checked by judgement. Experience tells us that society
cannot be maintained without the authority of magistrates and that
this authority falls into contempt where exact obedience is not paid
to it. Hence, Hume continues, the duties of allegiance and of keeping promises stand on the same foundation — they are necessary
for social life.

From these claims he derives his further claim that consent is
an unnecessary shuffle in a theory of political obligation. Consent
theorists, Hume claims, ask:

(1) Why are we bound to obey our government?
and answer: because

(2) We have promised to obey our government, and

(3) We are bound to keep our promises.

Hume challenges this argument by asking:

(4) Why should we keep our word?

and answers: because

(5) It is necessary for civilised life.

But, Hume continues, (5) is itself a sufficient answer to (1), so there is no need to derive an answer to (1) from (3) by means of a highly speculative act of promising. Hume concludes that both the obligation to obey one's government and to keep one's promises have the same foundation, i.e. that civilised life makes them necessary

Immediately following his attempted refutation of consent theory, Hume goes on to ask, '*But to whom is allegiance due, and who is our lawful sovereign?* ' (1964, p. 368). He answers that all of the following can give 'good title' to the 'throne':

(1) lawful succession;

(2) the will of the aristocracy or of the people;

(3) the will of the last occupant of the throne; and

(4) cession of a territory by 'the ancient proprietor, especially when joined by conquest' (1964, p. 368–71).

Hume sums up his views on political obligation by concluding that:

> The general obligation which binds us to government is the interest and necessities of society; and this obligation is very strong. The determination of it to this or that particular prince . . . is frequently more uncertain and dubious. Present possession has considerable authority in these cases, and greater than in private property, because of the disorders which attend all revolutions and changes in government (1964, p. 371).

In the above passage Hume clearly distinguishes between (a) the general obligation to accept government and (b) the determination of it to a particular prince. Once this distinction is appreciated, it becomes clear that Hume's attempt to refute consent theory involved a misunderstanding of it. This theory does not claim that consent provides a better explanation than utility of the general obligation to accept government (to the extent to which it does promote welfare) but that consent is the only basis to a 'good title' by a particular claimant to the office which carries political authority. Therefore, the theoretical step which consent theory makes in its consent move is not at all unnecessary; on the contrary, it is a move which Hume makes himself in asking what it is that gives particular individuals 'good title' to the 'throne'. Hence, the issue before Hume, and us, is not whether utility provides a better account of the general obligation to accept government than does consent, but whether the bases for a right to hold political office which Hume mentions are theoretically sounder than consent.[6]

Hume appears to have two arguments for an affirmative answer to this question. The first is that 'with regard to morals' there is no standard by which a controversy can be decided other than general opinion, and that the view that consent is the basis of political authority is repugnant to the common sentiments of mankind' (1964, p. 371). History has been unkind to this argument since it is a commonplace in liberal democracies that the authority of governments has something to do with the consent of the governed, even if few liberal democrats can give a coherent and defensible theoretical elaboration of this view and many political theorists reject it.

A second argument can perhaps be found in Hume's claim, already quoted, that where the determination of the general obligation to obey government to particular persons is uncertain, their 'present possession has considerable authority . . . because of the disorders which attend all revolutions and changes of government'. This is no longer a persuasive argument, if it ever was, since the general acceptance of its conclusion must encourage at least those potential usurpers and conquerers who are likely to succeed in overthrowing an existing government and since democracy solves the problem of changing government without 'disorders' in a way consistent with consent theory.

Hume distinguishes between the 'general obligation' which binds us to government and the 'determination of it to this or that particular prince'. He pursues the latter issue by asking '(b)ut to whom is allegiance due and who is our lawful sovereign?' And he answers this question by offering a number of conditions which he claims give 'good title' to the throne. Now it may be suggested that Hume is here claiming only that these conditions give a *legally* good title (make someone a *lawful* sovereign) not that they give a *morally* good title. And that, therefore, it is a mistake to contrast Hume's answers to the question of good title with the consent answer. For the former perhaps deal only with legal title while the latter deals with moral title.

The legal interpretation of Hume's remarks, however, is unlikely to be correct. First, the general obligation which binds us to government Hume certainly understands as a moral obligation. For it is an instance of the second of the two types of 'moral duties' which he distinguishes at the beginning of his presentation of the 'more philosophical refutation' of consent theory. Therefore, when Hume switches to discussing the determination of the general obligation to some particular prince, via some good title, he must still be discussing a moral, not merely a legal, issue. Second, the standard (viz. general opinion) which he offers for settling the 'controversy' between consent as giving good title to political authority and the conditions he mentions, he offers as a standard for settling *moral* controversies, not legal ones. And, finally, if his remarks about good title are taken as legal ones only, this would not save Hume; it would only leave him with a glaring gap in his theory of political obligation. For it is possible to ask not just whether someone has a legally good title to holding an office but also whether he has a morally good title.

Objections from insufficient freedom of consent

Even if it is granted that the last two objections overlook the precise and limited scope of consent theory, there are futher well-known objections which may be regarded as fatal to the theory as now understood. One group of such objections involves the claim that the consent said to create political obligation and authority cannot do so because, in the case of many citizens, their consent is not sufficiently free to create an obligation. Hume advances such an objection when he asks, rhetorically:

> Can we seriously say that a poor peasant or artisan has a free choice to leave his country, when he knows no foreign language or manners, and lives from day to day by the small wages which he acquires? (1964, p. 363.)

Woozley (1979), in discussing Socrates's version of consent theory, has provided the most careful and comprehensive restatement of this type of objection so far presented. Woozley's critical discussion of consent theory is a particularly suitable one to respond to since the version of the theory he attributes to Socrates is similar to that defended here, at least regarding the question whether consent is insufficiently free. For example, the consent in question is understood to consist in Socrates remaining within the city-state of Athens when he was free to leave it. It is Woozley's considered conclusion:

95

. . . that the model of the social contract is an unsatisfactory
one for explaining or clarifying obligation to obey the law;
we have either to find the obligation elsewhere or to abandon
the claim that most of us any longer have it (1979, p. 109).

He reaches this conclusion by the following line of thought. He notes
that an 'agreement . . . does have to be free to be . . . one by which
the party imposes on himself the obligation to fulfil the agreement'
(1979, p. 104). He then asks 'what is to count as being or not being
free, and about the spectrum of freedom — how free is free?' (1979,
p. 104). He does not explicitly answer these questions but, in
response to them, lists some conditions the absence of which would
'count heavily in favour of the thesis that Socrates was free in
agreeing to obey the law' (1979, p. 104). The conditions which *are*
absent in Socrates's case are:

    (1) legal restrictions on emigration;

    (2) legal restrictions on taking one's property into emigration;

    (3) being forced to agree to obey;

    (4) being tricked into the agreement to obey;

    (5) being given insufficient time to decide whether to agree to
obey.

However, Woozley continues, the absence of these conditions is
not sufficient to make Socrates's agreement to obey the law (by
remaining in Athens) free. The following further conditions must
also be absent:

    (6) bureaucratic obstruction to departure;

    (7) lack of somewhere else to go;

    (8) excessive (financial) cost of emigration;

    (9) excessive (personal and cultural) cost of emigration.

Woozley clearly thinks that, even if Socrates's putative agreement
to obey the law were free of all these extra conditions, the conduct
of most modern citizens is not.

He notes that the seventh condition, lack of somewhere else to
go, confronts almost all would-be emigrants today, since all existing
states have severe restrictions on immigration and there are, of
course, no habitable territories left on earth which are not under
the jurisdiction of some state. Hence 'the conduct of few people
anywhere today can be seen as implying a fully free agreement'
(1979, p. 106). For, even if they are legally free to *leave* the state in
which they live, they are not legally free to *enter* anywhere else.

Regarding the eighth condition he asserts that '(i)t is surely
grotesquely false to tell a man just released from gaol, without a

job and without funds, that, if he does not like the way things are managed here, he is free to go somewhere else' (1979, p. 107). In short, lack of money (as well as some other deficiencies) may make it literally impossible for some persons (e.g. Hume's poor ignorant peasant) to emigrate.

The ninth condition points to non-financial costs of emigration which do not make departure impossible, yet make it prohibitively costly. They involve 'breaks in family ties, and in cultural ties, and the wrench of leaving home for a strange place and an alien way of life' (1979, p. 107). Woozley asks, rhetorically, '(c)an we then really say of the man held back by all those ties to a place and a way of life to which he feels that he belongs that he is free to go — or as free as the man with no such ties?' (1979, p. 107.)

Woozley's statement of this case against consent theory is particularly valuable, since he recognises that the obligation to obey the law created by an agreement to obey, is one which can be over-ridden by other obligations (1979, p. 109–10), and one which can supplement other obligations to obey the law (1979, p. 96). In other words, Woozley appreciates the narrow scope of consent theory.

As noted, Woozley asks how free an agreement has to be to create an obligation, but does not explicitly answer the question. He responds by listing a number of conditions the presence of which would prevent an agreement from coming off. Therefore, his response to the question seems to be at least consistent with the Hartian approach adopted in Chapter 2. This approach is, that the best way of specifying whether a putative promise has been made by a sufficiently free choice is via a list of conditions (defeating conditions) which prevent a promise from coming off and, therefore, have to be absent for a putative promise to create an obligation. Woozley's response to the question whether Socrates's agreement to obey the law was sufficiently free presumably consists then in the nine conditions noted. (Though this need not be intended as a complete list of such conditions.) The presence of one or more of these conditions may prevent Socrates's putative agreement to obey from coming off and the absence of all of them (*assuming* the list to be complete) shows that the putative agreement does come off and, therefore, puts Socrates under an agreement obligation to obey the law.

Woozley does not explicitly distinguish between the *status quo* and the reform versions of consent theory. But he appreciates that many of the conditions listed need not apply in some (possible) states. He notes explicitly that the first seven conditions were not present in Socrates's case. Nor presumably was the eighth. However, he clearly thinks that at least the seventh and ninth conditions are present for most members of existing states, that therefore 'very few of mankind' now are free to leave their states to the extent Socrates was (1979, p. 108) and that, therefore, 'the model of the social contract is an unsatisfactory one for explaining or clarifying obligation to obey the law' (1979, p. 109).

Critics of consent theory can grant that some of the conditions, which prevent an agreement to obey the law from coming off, are not present in some states, and that it is therefore empirically realistic to claim that they could be removed in those states where they do obtain. Among the most important of the removable defeating conditions listed earlier are (1) legal restrictions on emigration (usually combined with (3), coercion, since the legal restrictions are bound to have sanctions attached to them) and (4), deception (as by government censorship and misinformation).

But such critics can go on to claim that there are other defeating conditions whose presence, at least in the modern world, is unavoidable. Here Woozley points to condition (7), the inability to leave because no other state permits entry, presumably assuming — quite rightly — that it is unrealistic to claim that most states can be made to adopt an open-entry policy in the foreseeable future. And Woozley points also to the ninth condition (the high cultural and personal cost of emigration) as one which is irremovably present for most persons in all states. (Simmons, 1979, pp. 95–100, also claims that the ninth condition is a fatal difficulty for the membership version of consent theory.) Hence, these critics of consent theory can claim that it is not possible to reform states, not even liberal democracies, in such a way that an agreement to obey the law, consisting in continued residence in a state, is free from all the conditions which prevent such an agreement from creating an obligation to obey the law.

This conclusion is one which Woozley clearly believes to apply to most citizens of contemporary states. That is, most citizens of contemporary liberal democracies would not be given entry for residence by states other than where they live and, even if they were permitted entry elsewhere, would have to pay a very high price through the severance of personal and cultural ties for leaving their home societies.

A question now arises, which is not asked by Woozley or Simmons. Do these conditions prevent the agreement to obey the law from coming off only among those who would rather leave their home state than agree to obey the law, or do they also prevent it from coming off among those who are quite happy to obey and have no thought of leaving? Only in the latter case is the objection from unfree agreement fatal to consent theory. For in states which are reasonably just and reasonably efficient, and believed by their citizens to be so, the vast majority of citizens will *not* wish to leave and will be prepared to agree to obey the law by accepting full citizenship in their home state. Of course, even in such states there is likely to be a small number who do not wish to agree to obey but agree nevertheless because of the two conditions, (7) and (9), mentioned. But this does not damage consent theory. For it is not a condition of the acceptability of the theory that it demonstrate the existence of an authority relation between every citizen of an authoritative state and that state (cf. Simmons, 1979, p. 35ff.). The reform version of the theory tries to make a good case for the claims (a) that within a liberal democratic political philosophy actual consent by Jack and Jean Smith is necessary for the state to have political authority over them and for them to have the correlative political obligation to obey the state, (b) that such consent-based political authority and obligation is possible in contemporary liberal democracies, at least if such states are reformed in ways which are possible here and now. The truth of (b) does not require that a state have political authority over every single person residing within its territory. The possibility of consent-based political obligation and political authority is a matter of degree. If most adults in contemporary liberal democracies cannot be under consent-based political authority then (b) is more false than true; but if it is only a very small proportion of such citizens, whose agreement to obey the state fails to come off (or who refuse to agree to obey without leaving), then this is not sufficient to undermine (b).

Perhaps it needs to be stressed that the version of consent theory defended here does not rely on majority consent in a way that is inconsistent with the claim, made throughout this book, that the basis of political authority and obligation is the actual personal consent of those under political authority. It is not now being claimed that if the majority in a state agree to obey the law, then the state has political authority over every member, even those who do not consent. The claim is merely that if the majority consent, then the state has political authority over this majority. The state is not claimed to have political authority over the minority who do not consent. The point being made, in the previous paragraph, is that the existence of such a minority, provided it is small enough, does not provide a damaging objection to consent theory. For, as already noted, it is not necessary for consent theory to demonstrate the existence of an authority relation between all citizens and their state.

Let us now consider how damaging to consent theory the objection from unfree agreement is, dealing first with conditions which cannot altogether be eliminated (7, 8, and 9) and then with conditions which, if they exist, could readily be eliminated (1 to 6).

Inability to leave home-state[7]

Assume that Jean Smith detests the politics of her home state, prefers emigration to agreeing to obey the law, but is literally unable to emigrate because she neither has nor can get the money needed to do so. If Smith 'agrees' to obey in these circumstances, does her putative agreement fail because the alternative she prefers, emigration, is not open to her? As already noted, whether her putative agreement comes off depends on whether there is any condition which prevents it from doing so. It is not immediately clear that there is any such condition. In another place (Beran, 1977) I considered subsuming the case under the defeating condition of coercion. On the face of it, such an attempt fails. We may say that C coerces V to do X if, and only if,

(1) C wants V to do X,

(2) C threatens V with harm unless V does X,

(3) V does X at least partly to avoid the threatened harm.

Now it seems Smith's agreement to obey the law, in the circumstances described, need not be coerced since, on the face of it, none of the defining conditions of coercion need be satisfied. We may contrast here real cases of coerced citizenship with the present case. The East German state does forbid emigration for most citizens, attaches severe sanctions to attempts to leave the state without permission and builds life-threatening barriers across the main escape routes from East Germany. Citizens of East Germany who prefer to leave, but stay because of the threat of harm if they try to leave, clearly are coerced to stay and their staying therefore cannot be said to involve an agreement to obey which comes off. Many other states, by contrast, have no laws against emigration. They do not threaten, and readily issues passports to, those who wish to leave. It seems, therefore, that a citizen of such a state (such as Australia or the United Kingdom), who agrees to obey because he does not have the money to leave, cannot claim he is coerced to stay and to agree to obey. Rather, he agrees to obey because he does not have the money to leave.

However, this assessment of the situation may be too superficial. It is noted later (Chapter 7, see 'Some necessary reforms') that the extent of consent-based political obligation among native-born citizens is maximised where, *inter alia*, there exists either a procedure for explicitly agreeing to obey the state when one has the opportunity to assume full political rights or a generally known convention to the effect that continued residence in a state, when one has this opportunity, counts as tacit consent to obey the state. Now assume the former alternative obtains. That is, when citizens cease to be political minors they must either explicitly agree to obey the state or leave. Further assume that a sanction (say, 6 months' gaol) is imposed on those who do neither. Now we can subsume Jean Smith's agreement to obey the law under the definition of coercion. For now the state does want her to agree to obey or leave the country, does threaten her with harm unless she does one or the other, and it will be the case (regarding some actual Jean Smith) that Smith agrees to obey, at least partly because of the sanction on non-agreement — given that she cannot leave because of lack of money.

So consent theory must acknowledge that in so far as:

(a) a state places sanctions on those who are within its borders without agreeing to obey its laws,

(b) there are persons within this state who wish to leave but cannot,

(c) such persons agree to obey the law at least partly because of the sanctions attached to not agreeing, consent-based political obligation and authority is not possible. Consent theory must grant that persons to whom conditions (a), (b) and (c) apply, are not under political authority or obligation.

The extent to which this admission damages consent theory depends on the proportion of citizens whose putative consent is prevented from coming off because conditions (a), (b) and (c) apply to them. Condition (b) will not apply to the vast majority of citizens in reasonably just and efficient states. For the vast majority of citizens in such states will be quite happy to become full citizens of their native states and to agree to obey their laws. (As already noted, consent theory is only committed to the possibility of consent-based political obligation and authority in states that are reasonably just and efficient. Furthermore, neither will condition (a) apply to native-born citizens if the form of consent in a state is tacit rather than express consent. For in this case the continued residence of native-born citizens, when they cease to be political minors, will count as tacit consent despite their inability to leave. And the issue of sanctions will arise only for the, presumably, even smaller minority who (a) cannot leave, (b) are not prepared to let their continued residence count as consent and, therefore, (c) explicitly reject membership by making a declaration to this effect to the appropriate officials. Therefore, the proportion of citizens to which the present objection unavoidably applies is so small that the objection does no significant damage to the reform version of consent theory. Implicit all along has been the admission that, in the foreseeable future, even in reasonably just and efficient states there is likely to be a small proportion of persons who would rather leave their state than agree to obey it, but who, for one reason or another (e.g. lack of money, health or knowledge), literally cannot at a given time.

It may be objected that there are or could readily be plausible cases of reasonably just and efficient states *most* of whose citizens want to emigrate but cannot. This could be the case if a very poor state neighbours a very rich state. It may well be the case that most of the citizens of some poor Pacific Ocean island state know enough about, say, the United States to want to migrate there, even if their own state is just and efficient. Yet their poverty may prevent them from doing so.

But if it is the case that the majority are prevented by poverty from leaving their home territory, then the case can no longer be subsumed under the defeating condition of coercion. For if we assume that the state in question has to be democratic in order to be reasonably just, then the majority has the right to abolish the state of which they are members. Therefore, while it may be true that they cannot leave the island in which they have grown up, they can leave the state of which they are citizens — by abolishing it. Therefore, it is not the case that they are coerced by the existing state to either agree to obey or leave it. Or, to put it differently, being the majority, if anyone is coercing them it is they themselves, and this is, of course, no coercion at all.

In case this reply somehow seems to miss the point of the objection, another response may be provided. Let it be the case that for one reason or another the inhabitants of a territory cannot leave it. If these people want to set up fair and efficient political institutions, surely they can mutually agree in a morally binding way to set up or to maintain such institutions even if it is the case that they would prefer to live in another place which, alas, they cannot reach.

It seems reasonable to conclude, therefore, that the admitted inability of some people to act on their wish to leave their home territory does not undermine the possibility of consent-based political obligation and authority. If the conditions (a), (b) and (c), mentioned above, apply to a person, then that person's agreement to obey the state is coerced and not morally binding. That person, therefore, is not under political authority or obligation. But because this situation applies only to a small proportion of the citizens of a reasonably just state, it does not undermine consent theory. If it is true of a substantial minority that they cannot leave their home territory, then often it will not be true that they cannot leave the state of which they are members, for they would be able to leave it by secession rather than by the admittedly impossible step of emigration. And if it is true of a majority of the citizens of a state that they cannot leave their home territory, then it is not true that they cannot leave their state for they could abolish it. Hence, in the latter two cases these people's inability to leave their home territory does not inevitably involve them in being coerced to agree to obey the law of their state. Of course such people may be coerced by their fellow citizens to remain part of the existing state by being prevented by force from seceding or abolishing the existing state. But then, normally, such a state would not be a reasonably just one and consent theory is not committed to the claim that consent-based political obligation and authority is possible in a state which is not reasonably just.

Denial of entry elsewhere

As Woozley points out (1979, pp. 105–6), inability to leave one's home state can be due to conditions which are internal or external to one's home state. It may be due to poverty or the refusal of other states to grant entry for residence (combined with the lack of habitable territories not under the jurisdiction of some state). The special significance of this external condition preventing emigration rests in it being likely to apply to most citizens of most states. Moreover, it is unrealistic to assume that states in the future will significantly reduce present barriers against entry of foreigners for residence. If the mere inability to leave one's home state prevented an agreement to obey it from coming off, then consent theory would be untenable. But inability to leave one's home state has to be combined with a desire to leave before the issue of one's agreement to obey the state not coming off arises.

The external constraint denying entry elsewhere no more under-
mines consent theory than do internal constraints, such as poverty.
The vast majority of citizens of reasonably fair and efficient states
will be happy to agree to obey the law and will not want to leave
their home states. Some of the substantial minorities which may
wish to leave even such a state (e.g. an ethnic minority which desires
self-government) may be sufficiently concentrated territorially to
leave their home state by secession rather than emigration. (Politically speaking, new Americas can often be found *within* America.)
If the majority in a state disapprove of the existing government or
of the existing political arrangement, they can try to reach agreement on preferred alternatives and, being the majority, they would
be able to bring them about. Of the individuals who do not wish
to agree to obey the existing state, some *will* be permitted entry for
residence into other states. No doubt this will leave some to whom
the conditions (a), (b) and (c) listed above (p. 101) do apply and
whose putative agreement to obey is, therefore, coerced and,
therefore, does not come off. However, since we are now considering people who have the means to leave their home state and who
are stopped from doing so only by the lack of somewhere else to
go, their difficulty can be removed by existing states creating a
number of dissenters' territories, i.e. territories created by the
adjustment of existing borders and kept outside the jurisdiction of
states, where those who do not wish to agree to obey the states in
which they find themselves can move. Hence, the admittedly severe
restrictions on immigration which most if not all existing states have
and are likely to maintain in the future do not undermine consent
theory.

In conclusion, the inability to act on the wish to leave the state in
which one lives (because of conditions internal or external to that
state), cannot be subsumed under the defeating condition of coercion, except in so small a proportion of the citizens that it does not
undermine consent theory. This leaves open the possibility that the
inability to leave one's state can be subsumed under some defeating
condition other than coercion or that it is a defeating condition in
its own right. There appears to be no plausible candidate other than
coercion under which this inability might be subsumed. Nor is it
plausible to insist (not on any argument known by this author) that
inability to leave one's state is a defeating condition in its own right.

The high cost of emigration

Assume that Jack Smith detests the politics of his home state, that his home state requires him either to agree to obey the law or leave and that he agrees to obey the law because, although he could emigrate, he does not wish to do so, because he finds the prospect of leaving homeland, friends and relatives intolerable. Woozley suggests that such a person's agreement to obey the law is not sufficiently free to create an obligation to obey (1979, p. 107).

As already noted, the question whether Jack Smith is free enough for his agreement to come off, is to be answered by considering whether the high price he would have to pay for not agreeing prevents his agreement to obey from coming off. Consider these cases. Green has an illness which is fatal unless dealt with in hospital. Hospitals require that patients agree to observe their rules while there. Green not only dislikes being in hospital as such but also objects to being bound by rules in whose making he had no say. Does Green's (reluctant) agreement to observe the hospital rules not come off because the alternative to agreeing is certain death? Brown, who is wealthy and detests lawyers, has been arrested on a charge of murder but is innocent. She has so little knowledge of the law and court procedures that she is likely to be convicted unless she hires an attorney. Does her agreement to pay standard legal fees to the attorney not come off because the likely cost of not agreeing to this is conviction of murder? According to received moral opinion, the answer in both cases is no. Moreover, received opinion probably has wisdom on its side here. If the severe predicaments in which Green and Brown find themselves prevented them from placing themselves under agreement obligations, then they would find it more difficult to get help to overcome their predicaments. For they could not enter into the sort of mutual agreements (if you agree to provide me with legal services, I agree to pay a reasonable fee) that may get them out of their difficulties. In short, being able to place oneself under a promissory obligation even when one does not want to and when the only alternative involves a high cost, may still increase the options available to one in a problem-situation. Therefore, in the sense of 'free' in which the more options one has the more free one is, being able to place oneself under a promissory obligation in situations such as those discussed increases one's freedom. One may conclude, therefore, that the high price involved in not agreeing to do something is not a defeating condition of promising, even if the promise in question is one which one is reluctant to make.

105

The plausibility of this conclusion is even clearer in light of the following. If G is reluctant to agree to do X, but agrees to do it nevertheless, because he knows the alternative is to accept a high price, it follows neither that G has been coerced into agreeing to do X, nor that G, in agreeing to do X, has been exploited. It does not follow that G has been coerced into agreeing to do X; for the high price on not agreeing to do X may not be one which is intentionally imposed by some persons in order to make G agree to do X. Such imposition is an instance of coercion and coercion is, of course, a defeating condition of putative promising. Nor does it follow that G, in agreeing to do X, is being exploited. The fee which the barrister is charging Brown in the example used above may be an entirely fair one. This point is important since, if the barrister were the only one available to Brown and made his defence of Brown conditional on an exploitative fee being paid, then Brown's reluctant agreement to pay the fee may not come off. For exploitation is a defeating condition of putative promises.

The agreement to obey the state (which is the ultimate focus of the present discussion), the alternative to which involves the high price of losing personal and cultural relationships, need involve neither coercion nor exploitation. For a government, in insisting that a citizen either agree to obey the state or leave, need not be using the potential loss of these relationships as a weapon to extract such an agreement. And though governments may know that citizens who do not wish to agree to obey the state may be faced with the dilemma of agreeing to obey or losing personal and cultural ties, such governments, in insisting that citizens agree to obey or depart, need not be exploiting their citizens' predicaments. For their insistence that one of the alternatives be chosen may be entirely justified.

So far I have been considering only the more plausible objection according to which the high price of emigration or the inability to emigrate defeats a putative agreement to obey the state *only if the citizen concerned wishes to emigrate.* My reply has been, basically, that in a reasonably just state, this objection does not apply to a high enough proportion of citizens to undermine consent theory. This objection would apply to a much higher proportion of citizens if the 'wishes to leave clause' of the objection were dropped. In other words, if it were claimed that a putative promise does not come off unless there exists an alternative to promising which is not highly detrimental to the potential promiser; and that this is so whether the potential promiser wishes to make the promise or not.

Woozley (1979) and Simmons (1979) — who state the present type of objection to consent theory from insufficiently free consent most fully — do not make the distinction between the more and the less plausible interpretation of this type of objection. No one, as far as I know, has explicitly put forward the less plausible version of the objection, a fact perhaps sufficient in itself to show that there is no case to answer. But it seems extremely unlikely in any case that a good case can be made for this less plausible objection. Take the high-price-of-non-agreement condition first. The hypothetical legal case of Brown and the medical case of Green show that, according to received moral opinion, a putative agreement *can* come off despite the disastrous price attached to non-agreement, even though the potential agreers are loath to make the agreement. Hence it is hardly likely that a good argument can be produced to show that such putative agreements *cannot* come off in cases in which the potential agreers *do* wish to make the agreement. Next let us return to the inability-to-leave condition. It is clear that if the person who cannot leave the state in which he lives *does* wish to agree to obey the state concerned, then this agreement to obey cannot be coerced. For one is not coerced to do X, if one does X because one wants to do X, rather than because of a threat of harm unless one does X.

The other defeating conditions

We now return, briefly, to the other conditions which Woozley lists as undermining consent theory: (1) legal restrictions on emigration or (2) on taking one's property into emigration, (3) coercion, (4) deception, (5) insufficient time to decide whether to agree to obey the state and (6) bureaucratic obstacles to emigration. Clearly none of these conditions need apply widely enough in contemporary liberal democracies to create difficulties for consent theory. Nor is it implausible, within a liberal democratic framework, to claim, as consent theory does, that the presence of these conditions can prevent or destroy the existence of an authority relation between a state and its citizens. For example, it is not implausible to claim that if some citizens have agreed to obey a state as a result of coercion or deception, then this state does not have political authority over them and they do not have that particular obligation to obey this state which is the correlative of political authority.

I doubt whether any contemporary writers would wish to

107

disagree with the above claims. But Hume certainly did, for he wrote:

> And did a prince observe, that many of his subjects were seized with a frenzy of migrating to foreign countries, he would doubtless, with great reason and justice, restrain them, in order to prevent the depopulation of his Kingdom. Would he forfeit the allegiance of all his subjects, by so wise and reasonable a law? Yet the freedom of their choice is surely, in that case, ravished from them. (1964, p. 364.)

So Hume would not accept that citizens, who are coerced and legally constrained to remain within a state they do not wish to be in, thereby cease to be under political obligation. But his argument for this claim appeals to received moral opinion; and even if such opinion provided a good base for the argument in Hume's day, it does so no longer, not at least among consistent liberal democrats. According to the United Nations Universal Declaration of Human Rights, people have the moral right to leave their country permanently and to change their nationality and should have the corresponding legal rights. Now, if people are forcibly denied the exercise of the moral right to leave the state of which they are citizens, then surely it is not implausible to claim that they cease to be under political obligation. Or at least it is not implausible to claim this, provided that they have not put themselves under some special obligation which they cannot fulfil if they leave, that they have not broken the law and not yet met the penalty, and that their leaving is compatible with the government fulfilling its constitutional functions.

It seems fair to conclude that there is only a small proportion of citizens of liberal democracies whose (possible) agreement to obey the state would inevitably fail to come off because of the presence of certain practically irremovable conditions. For the vast majority of citizens, consent-based political obligation and authority is not made impossible by insufficiently free consent.

Consent not a necessary condition of political obligation

According to the membership version of consent theory, the consent which creates political obligation and authority consists, for native-born citizens, in acceptance of full membership in the state when they cease to be political minors. Now whether such consent is express or tacit, consent theory must acknowledge that such consent cannot come off unless there is something which it is possible to do which counts as refusing to consent to obey. One such action, which is open even to someone who is unable to leave the state in which he lives, is a public declaration to the appropriate officials, say at the time when he ceases to be a political minor, that he is not accepting membership in the state. Such action must be possible for consent theory to be tenable, and someone who makes such a declaration, in the appropriate way, is not under political obligation or authority.

This admission does not reduce consent theory to absurdity for at least two reasons. First, if some people neither agree to obey the state in which they live nor emigrate nor secede, then the state may be justified in expelling them to the dissenters' territory the creation of which was mooted earlier in this chapter.[8] Second, if the state does not expel them, then they continue to live within its territory, and yet are not under political obligation.[9] However, they would still be morally required to act in accordance with the law in many cases because of moral reasons for doing what is legally required which are independent of the political authority of the state over a particular citizen. One is not morally justified in killing people just because one is not under political obligation not to do so. One is morally required to observe sensible traffic laws even in a deeply unjust tyranny.

While the admission just made again reveals the narrow scope of consent theory, this narrow scope does not trivialise it. Let P be someone who lives in a given state but is not under political obligation to it. What difference does this absence of political obligation make to the justification of political action? If one is under political obligation then there is an exclusionary defeasible reason for obeying the law. Hence there is one reason for obeying the law for those who are under political obligation which does not hold for P. Hence P may be morally justified in disobeying the law in some cases where those who are under political obligation would not be. For example, assume that there is a law against doing X and there are no moral reasons for or against doing X independent of the possible political obligation to do X. (States do ban some actions which are not morally wrong.) Then those who are under political obligation have a moral reason against doing X, no moral reasons for doing X, and, therefore, ought, morally speaking, not to do X. P, on the other hand, is not under political obligation, and, therefore, it is morally indifferent whether P does X.

Next (it may be objected) if the political obligation and authority creating consent for native-born citizens consists in accepting full membership in the state when people cease to be political minors, what can this version of consent theory say about the political obligation of political minors? A difficulty arises most clearly for the membership version of consent theory, if it is the case that there is some age, say fourteen, at which adolescents, while sufficiently mature to be under a moral obligation to obey the law, are not sufficiently mature to choose their place of residence; hence they would not have the moral or legal right to emigrate without the consent of their legal guardians. Hence, such adolescents, prevented from emigration by coercion, would not be under political obligation and authority. Consent theory may have to accept this conclusion. But alternatively, it appears to be possible to legitimately qualify the theory as follows.

With regard to some terms, it is possible to distinguish between a paradigm and an extended use, or between central and peripheral cases falling under the term. It was argued earlier, following Brandt (1964), that this distinction can be applied to the concepts of *obligation* and *duty*. (Chapter 2, see 'Natural and institutional morality'.) Some writers express this distinction as one between logically primary and logically secondary cases falling under a concept. D.M. Armstrong offers a very precise definition of 'logically secondary'.

It is clear that Armstrong's definition applies only to some of the terms regarding which it is plausible to distinguish between a paradigm and an extended use. But this is not a good objection to his definition, since there is no reason to think that the distinction between paradigm and extended use of a term or between central (or primary) and peripheral (or secondary) cases falling under a concept must always follow the same logical pattern.

Armstrong defines 'logically secondary' thus:

> Let it be given that there is a class of things of the sort X, and a sub-class of X: the class of things Y. Y's are then logically secondary instances of X if, and only if, (i) it is logically possible that there should be no Y's and yet there still be X's; but (ii) it is logically impossible that Y's should be the only X's which exist (1973, p. 28.)

If this definition of 'logically secondary' is tenable then the political obligation of political minors is a logically secondary instance of political obligation. For it is logically impossible for all the members of the class 'persons who are under political obligation to state S' to be political minors; if this were so there could not be a state S (though there could be a society S not politically organised) since, by definition, political minors cannot fill the positions which must be filled for a state to exist. On the other hand, it is logically possible that this class should consist of full members only. I have some doubt whether it is appropriate to apply the distinction between logically primary and logically secondary cases falling under a concept to political obligation but will tentatively do so. Hence, the claim that consent is a necessary condition of political obligation and authority within liberal democratic theory, has to be qualified thus: consent is a necessary condition of political obligation and authority in logically primary cases. This qualification is to be understood as required whenever consent is claimed (in this book) to be a necessary condition of political obligation and authority.

Another objection to the identification of consent with voluntary acceptance of membership is raised by Casinelli (1961, p. 92). He contends that the relationship between an association and its members is 'truly voluntary' only when the members can take themselves beyond its control 'at any time whatsoever'. But, Casinelli notes, citizens are not allowed to withdraw from their government's control if they have broken the law (and not yet met the penalty for such violation). Therefore, he concludes, the relation between citizen and state cannot be truly voluntary and consent cannot consist in (continued) voluntary acceptance of membership in the state.

We may put to one side Casinelli's claim that an association is 'truly voluntary' only if its members can leave it 'at any time whatsoever', even if they have broken the rules of the association and not yet met the penalty for such infringement. However, it is important to show that membership in the state is voluntary enough for acceptance of such membership to give rise to political obligation and authority, even if the legal right to leave the state is subject to three qualifications. These are that the legal right to leave may not be exercisable if:

    (1) the citizen has broken the law and not yet met the penalty for doing so;

    (2) the citizen has incurred any special obligations he cannot fulfil if he leaves;

    (3) the citizen's leaving undermines the government's ability to fulfil its constitutional functions.

Examples of (1) are obvious — perhaps the citizen has committed fraud and been sentenced to a year's gaol which he has not yet served. An example of (2) is someone who has signed an agreement with the government that he will serve as a doctor in the country for five years as a condition of receiving medical training which is subsidised by tax-payers to the tune of 60,000 dollars. Under (3) citizens may be prohibited from emigrating while their state is at war.

Now consider a citizen who, on ceasing to be a political minor, accepts full membership in the state, thereby agrees to obey the state, and thereby puts himself under an obligation to obey the state. Obviously, this includes not just an obligation to obey the law but also one to accept whatever sanctions are attached to breaking the law and an obligation to accept any (legal) requirements the government places on the citizen to fulfil its constitutional functions; and, *ex hypothesi* these are self-assumed obligations arising from the citizen's agreeing to obey the state in the absence of any conditions which would have prevented this agreement from coming off. Sometime after accepting membership, such a citizen may wish to leave his state before, say, meeting a penalty for breaking a law and perhaps indeed in order to avoid meeting this penalty. The state is likely to prevent such departure by force in order to be able to enforce the penalty in question. It would then be the case that the citizen remaining in the state is coerced. But it would, nevertheless, also be the case that he is under a self-assumed obligation to accept the penalty for his law infringement. Analogous considerations apply to the other cases. Therefore, consent-based political obligation and authority is compatible with the three qualifications to the legal right to emigrate and, even where consent is understood to consist in acceptance of membership in the state, does not require a right to leave 'at any time whatsoever'. Acceptance of membership in a state should be revocable within a liberal democratic theory of the state. For persons cannot predict with certainty what is in their long-term interest. As Frederic Schick notes in his 'Towards a Logic of Liberalism', '(c)ontracts in perpetuity . . . must be watched with particular care and must always be cancellable' (1980, p. 44). But such revocation can, consistently with the present version of consent theory, be subject to the three qualifications mentioned.

However, this reply to Casinelli's objection makes an assumption which he could rightly challenge and the dropping of which does require a further, but non-fatal, acknowledgement of the limits of consent theory. The argument assumes that a citizen will not

112

find himself in the kind of situation referred to in the three qualifications without having had the option of declining to be a member
of the state. But this need not be so. Assume that full citizenship
and the legal right to emigrate without permission of one's parents
is granted at the age of eighteen. Now assume also that the law allows
natural parents below this age to take responsibility for their
children. Such parents fall under qualification (2) for they have
assumed special legal responsibilities (i.e. responsibilities which
citizens do not have simply *qua* citizen). Therefore, if, on turning
eighteen, such a parent decided, by emigration, to reject membership in the state in which he has grown up, and also to reject responsibility for bringing up the children produced, the state may deny
emigration and treat the parent as a member of the state until
appropriate arrangements for the children's welfare have been made.
Here we would have an instance of someone who falls under one
of the three qualifications to the legal right of emigration — but
someone who has not agreed to be bound by these qualifications.
Consent theory has to grant that if such a person remains in the
state due to coercion then this person is not under political obligation or authority.

The difficulty for the emigrant *manqué* is, of course, not
insuperable. He would gain permission to exercise his right to
emigrate, if he makes appropriate arrangements for the welfare of
his children, which could be, *inter alia*, that they are looked after by
the other parent (perhaps with his guaranteed financial support)
or taken abroad by him. Or if there is no one else that can take
responsibility for the children, and it is not possible for him to take
them abroad, then he may decide not to emigrate after all and to
accept membership in the state in which he has grown up. If he
declines to emigrate for this reason, rather than from fear of government sanctions, then his agreement to obey the state can of course
come off.

Still, consent theory must grant that any given time there are
bound to be some persons, even in the most just states practically
achievable in the foreseeable future, who will be deemed members
of the state because they fall under one or more of the three qualifications to the right of emigration mentioned, but without their prior
consent. Such persons may not be under political obligation. But,
once again, it can be plausibly asserted that the proportion of citizens
of whom this is true is likely to be too small to destroy the claim
that consent-based political obligation and authority is possible.

At times of special stress in a society, a state may prohibit emigration of more considerable numbers of citizens who have not agreed to obey the state. The most obvious case is a state which, in the course of war, does not permit citizens to exercise their right of emigration. Such denial may be justified by the state's function of defending its citizens. This denial of the exercise of the right of emigration may include a denial to those who cease to be political minors during the war. Such persons, to the extent to which they are coerced to be members of the state during the war, would not be under political obligation. If the state is fighting a just war, a high proportion of citizens who cease to be political minors would presumably accept membership in the state without coercion. Still, the present case could involve greater numbers of citizens who are coerced to be members than the previous case discussed. On the other hand, the present case would arise only on relatively rare occasions. Therefore, the present case also only qualifies the possibility of consent-based political obligation without undermining it.

John Finnis (1984) denies on two grounds that consent is necessary for political authority. The first is that consent theory is one of 'the theories . . . which tacitly assume that the present authority of particular rulers must rest on some prior authority . . . of the community over itself, granted away to the ruler by transmission . . . or of the individual over himself, granted away by promise or implied contract or "consent" ' (1984, p. 247). This claim, to a prior authority of the community over itself, or the individual over himself, Finnis regards as 'intrinsically implausible' (1984, p. 248).

Whatever force this objection has against theories which make the claim noted by Finnis, it has none against the version of consent theory defended here. The present theory attributes no 'prior authority' to the community over itself or of the individual over himself. Nor is there any need for consent theory to do so. People do have a moral right to determine their political relationships and they can *create* (not transmit) political authority by agreeing to comply with the decisions of certain individuals. Perhaps this point needs repeating. Political authority (and authority-over in general) is not something which individuals or groups have prior to entering political relationships and which they transmit when making such an entry. Rather, it is something which is created by entering political relationships under certain conditions. This creation may involve the transfer of a right, but not the transfer of authority.

Finnis's second objection is that consent is not

. . . needed to constitute the state of affairs which (presumptively) justifies someone in claiming and others in acknowledging his authority to settle co-ordination problems for a whole
community by creating authoritative rules or issuing
authoritative orders and determinations. Rather, the required
state of facts is this: that in the circumstances the say-so of
this person or configuration of persons probably will be, by
and large, complied with and acted upon, to the exclusion of
any rival say-so and notwithstanding any differing preferences
of individuals about what should be stipulated and done in
the relevant fields of co-ordination problems (1984, p. 248–9).

It seems quite clear that Finnis is not here offering a general justification of authority as such, but making a claim about what makes
it appropriate for *particular* persons to claim that *they* are the holders
of this authority. This is clear from the way the claim quoted above
is repeated:

The sheer fact that virtually everyone *will* acquiesce in
somebody's say-so is the presumptively necessary and
defeasibly sufficient condition for the normative judgement
that that person has . . . authority in that community. (p. 250.)

Finnis's claim, that consent is not needed to constitute political
authority, is unsupported except by his own highly controversial
definition of authority. It therefore begs the question against those
who reject this definition. And there is a reason for rejecting it which
is accepted by most writers on political authority, including those
who reject consent theory, viz. that Finnis's account of political
authority seems to make it impossible to distinguish between power
and authority. If the sheer fact of acquiescence is sufficient to constitute authority then it is not at all clear how one could distinguish
between authority (a normative relationship) and power (an
empirical one).

Consent proves too much

While the last few objections cast doubt on consent being necessary
for political authority, the next three claim that consent theory proves
too much. John McCloskey has, in conversation, raised this possibility in the following way. Consent theory insists that consent-

based political obligation is a moral obligation. Hence, someone who is under such an obligation must have a moral obligation to observe traffic regulations even if he knows there is no possible point in doing so, say, because he knows he is travelling on a desert highway under conditions which make it perfectly safe to drive faster than at the prescribed speed limit. Surely, it is implausible to claim that such a traveller is under a *moral* obligation to do something which is entirely pointless, i.e. to waste time in driving more slowly than it is perfectly safe to do.

The difficulty McCloskey poses can be met by pointing to a feature of promissory obligation that has not yet been noted here. The need to fulfil such an obligation can become temporarily suspended even though one is able to fulfil the obligation. This can be the case where it is pointless or counterproductive to try to fulfil it. This is different from such an obligation being overridden by others or ceasing to exist. Consider this example. I promise my sister on her death-bed to bring up her young daughter. Some years after I start doing so, relations between me and my niece break down and she will have nothing to do with me. However, there is reasonable hope that she will in due course return to my household and for the present a neighbouring family, which has befriended her, is happy to treat her as part of their family and temporarily accept responsibility for her. In this case my promissory obligation to take care of the child does not cease nor is it overridden by any other obligation; moreover, I have the ability to fulfil the obligation, but it would be pointless and counterproductive to do so. It seems best to speak of the promissory obligation here being temporarily suspended. The same is the case in the traffic rules example, precisely because it would be pointless (and wasteful) to fulfil the obligation.

A more common attempt to show that consent theory proves too much, relies on the possibility, and all too frequently the actuality, of immoral laws. As Benn and Peters put it, if consent puts one under an obligation to obey the constitution and all valid laws, then one may be morally committed to obey immoral laws and accept laws which oppress minorities (1969, p. 323). The reply to this objection can take one of two forms, depending on whether it is possible to promise to do something that is morally wrong. If it is not, then the objection does not get off the ground. Some writers claim that a promise to do something morally wrong does not come off (or at least does not create an obligation to do the promised act). If this approach is sound, then the immorality of an act one attempts to promise to do can be added to the list of conditions (stated in Chapter 2, see 'Consent'), which prevent a promise from coming off. If a putative promise to do something immoral can come off, then a different reply to the present objection is available. The consent to an immoral law may then create an obligation to obey it. On the other hand, the immorality of the particular law in question will also provide a reason against obeying it. If the law is grossly immoral, then the reason against compliance may override the political obligation to obey.

The present line of thought can readily be applied to oppressed minorities. In existing liberal democracies, many members of such minorities are alienated from political institutions and largely so because they feel disadvantaged, oppressed and powerless. The disadvantages often include educational ones. The epistemological objection to the *status quo* version of actual consent theory (few citizens understand that residence *counts* as tacit consent, therefore it cannot *be* tacit consent) applies most obviously to such alienated 'citizens'. They least of all can be claimed to tacitly consent to obey the state through their residence in it. It is far more plausible to say that they lack the interest in and understanding of the political institutions required for attributing tacit consent to them and that they, therefore, are not under political obligation or authority.

Such 'citizens' are also least likely to have institutional obligations to obey the state from the other two sources of such obligations identified in Chapter 5. They are most likely to abstain from democratic elections or to vote with too little understanding of the function of elections for their voting to place them under an obligation to accept the outcome of the election. And since they are members of an oppressed minority it is not easy to make judgements about the extent, if any, to which they benefit from the law-abidingness of their fellow citizens.

So, for oppressed minorities, the moral reasons for obeying the law are most likely to be those of natural morality. Whether they exist will depend on the content of individual laws. No doubt oppressed minorities are morally required to comply with sensible traffic laws. Equally clearly, they have no moral reasons to comply with laws which directly oppress them. The case for obeying the rest of their state's laws has to be treated on the merits of each law as it confronts the member of the oppressed minority, but in the absence of any political obligation to obey it.

In the next chapter, measures are proposed which would (a) ensure that all persons born into a state know that continued

117

residence in it counts as tacit consent, and (b) maximise the proportion of citizens whose putative consent is free from defeating conditions and, therefore, puts them under political obligation. But in such a state there could still be oppressed minorities. Members of such a minority may prefer to accept membership in the state in which they have grown up despite their unjust treatment. They may wish most of all to live in their home state without being oppressed, but they may also prefer being oppressed citizens in their home state to emigration or secession or life in a dissenters' territory. However, if such citizens do consent to obey the laws of their home state, including those which are unjust to them, then in line with the two alternatives stated above, either they are not under political obligation to obey unjust laws or, if they are, the immorality of these laws may override their political obligation to obey them and may justify disobedience.

Finally, the suggestion that consent theory proves too much may raise the following question. Are persons, who have a right of personal self-determination, under political obligation and authority in a state which makes membership genuinely voluntary (and insists on consent or departure), but in which governments are self-perpetuating dictatorships instead of being democratically selected? This, in fact, is only a variation on a question put by John McCloskey: Are the citizens of South American dictatorships which freely permit emigration under consent-based political obligation? In other words, does the right of self-determination require, not only that membership in the state be voluntary, but also that the internal political decision-making of the state be democratic?

This question has already been answered in the affirmative. In Chapter 5 (see 'The democracy version') it is claimed that circumstances can perhaps be imagined in which persons with a right of self-determination may temporarily prefer not to exercise this right (e.g. in times of civil or foreign war). But, in normal circumstances, only a democratic political decision-making procedure is compatible with a right of personal self-determination. Hence, if a minority (the hypothetical dictators and their supporters) imposes an undemocratic method of government selection on the majority, this imposition is, at least normally, grossly unjust. Therefore, the consent involved in accepting membership in this state is consent, *inter alia*, to a grossly unjust method of government selection. So, once again, we have to say either that the injustice of these laws defeats the putative consent from coming off (from creating an obligation) or, if the consent does come off, that the resulting obligation to comply with the unjust laws is overridden by their being grossly unjust.

Consent-based political obligation undesirable

We turn, finally, to objections which do not challenge the possibility of consent-based political obligation but its desirability. Karen Johnson claims that the voluntary association model of the state trivialises membership in it. She thinks this is so since:

> If the obligations of membership begin to weigh too heavily upon him (i.e. the citizen) he can exercise his option to resign. Thus he is never likely to be in a position as a member where he has to do something he really does not want to do. In the voluntary association model, therefore, the problem of political obligation tends to evaporate (1975, p. 20).

She adds that the voluntary association model of political obligation is not a suitable ideal since in placing high value on the right to emigrate, it places a lower value on participation. Johnson's argument seems to echo and develop Burke's claim (1975) that the state ought not to be considered as nothing better than an agreement to run a lowly trading company to be abandoned at will, but as a partnership in science, virtue and perfection between the living, the dead and those yet to be born.

Johnson's objection clearly applies to the present version of consent theory. In identifying consent with accepting membership in the state, the present theory is committed to the view that a state which has political authority is a voluntary association.[10] It is also worth noting that Johnson's objection is incompatible with the starting point of the Woozley/Simmons objection to the possibility of consent-based political obligation from the high personal and cultural cost of emigration. While the Woozley/Simmons objection is shown to be unsound, it remains that, for most citizens, emigration does involve a great loss of friendship, family, culture and association with scenes of the triumphs and tragedies of their own past. This means that even citizens who are dissatisfied with the policies of their government, or with the form which political activity takes in their state, will be reluctant to emigrate. Whether or not citizens who are dissatisfied with the politics of their state are likely to participate in attempts to change policies or forms of political activity, most will be reluctant to take up the option of exit. In short, as Pateman notes, '(l)eaving . . . some voluntary associations, such as churches or political parties, can be a major and devastating step in an individual's life' (1979, p. 96). Clearly, to leave one's state, even if conceived as a voluntary association, would prove a great loss. Finally, it may be noted that, while Johnson extols the virtues of states which are compulsory associations with regard to membership, she fails to say whether she is in favour of liberal democracies abolishing the legal right to emigration which exists, at least by convention, in most if not all of them.

J.F.M. Hunter casts doubts on the desirability of having a continuing social contract on two grounds. He claims that 'it would appear to ossify the social structure unduly, by making basic changes impossible without elaborate contract negotiations'. He makes the further objection that 'neither citizens nor governments would gain from it anything of value which they did not already possess or which could be achieved only in this way' (1966, p. 36–7).

The first difficulty is not a serious one for the present version of consent theory, since it is entirely compatible with the possibility of constitutional change. Any adequate constitution will include a procedure for changing it. The device most obviously in the spirit of consent theory is constitutional change by popular referendum with citizens having the legal right to initiate such a referendum if a sufficient number of them demand it.

In reply to Hunter's second objection, we may return to claims already made in Chapter 4 against utilitarian liberalism. In brief, only consent-based political obligation and authority can adequately satisfy the moral right of persons to self-determination. This reply can be elaborated in terms of the distinction between natural obligations and agreement-obligations to obey the state. It is the natural obligations to obey which are the primary reasons for accepting the proper requirements of the state. For only if there are good moral reasons for having states and complying with their requirements, can there be any good moral reason for putting oneself under an agreement-obligation to obey the state. But agreement-obligations to comply remain indispensible to a theory of political obedience, because the state and its political arrangements and laws are not natural phenomena unchangeable by human effort. What political institutions to have, how many states to have, what policies to pursue: these are not matters given to humanity by nature, but are matters determined by human decision. Therefore, only once such human decisions have been turned into political institutions and policies, is there something that can be complied with. And only if such arrangements are made by voluntary human agreements is the moral right of persons to self-determination satisfied.

One more objection remains to be considered. Chapter 4 discusses and rejects the view — attributed to utilitarian and hypothetical consent liberalism — that a natural duty or obligation to obey the state is by far the most important element in a liberal democratic theory of justified political obedience and that actual consent is an inessential or inappropriate element in such a theory. This view is objected to on the ground that it is fatally incomplete, since it cannot provide an adequate account of the basis of political authority.

John Kilkullen (personal communication) has challenged the line of argument in Chapter 4, as follows: even if one grants that the state is needed to co-ordinate some of the activities of its citizens, one does not have to grant that the state needs political authority in the sense used by me (i.e. not just as *legal* authority, but as authority which involves a *moral* right to compliance with the law). Such authority is not needed, he claims, since, if a particular law is justified, citizens have a natural duty to comply with it and, if it is not justified, it is best if citizens do not have any moral reason to comply with it.

This objection can be met by showing that natural duty is not sufficient as an account of reasons for action in the political realm. A liberal democratic theory of politics has to construct (*inter alia*) a theory of political decision-making which explains how political decisions can be made which are normally morally binding on all citizens, despite the fact that unanimity is impossible. An adequate theory of politics has to propose a decision-making procedure which can normally yield decisions which create sufficient reasons for compliance despite disagreements over ends, over the ranking of ends and over appropriate means of achieving them. Reliance on a natural duty (or obligation) to comply with just (or utility-maximising) laws is not enough. For with regard to many decisions, there will be some citizens who believe the decision is one they do not have a natural duty to obey and other citizens who are uncertain whether the decision is one they have a natural duty to obey. Yet, given that decisions have to be made in the face of disagreements, the mere fact that one is not sure whether one has a natural duty to comply with a particular law or the mere fact that one believes that one does not have a natural duty to comply cannot be sufficient to justify non-compliance. For a liberal democrat has to acknowledge that he has to comply with *some* decisions he believes to be wrong. A natural duty to comply with decisions which are just or utility-maximising is not sufficient to explain this fact of liberal-democratic life.

The problem of how to create morally binding decisions in the face of disagreement can be solved by creating political authority, i.e. authority which involves a moral right to compliance with its decisions. For the decisions of such authority create a reason for complying with it which is independent of the substantive merits of the decision. And this reason may provide a sufficient reason for compliance for someone who is uncertain about the substantive merits of the decision and also for someone who thinks there are no substantive reasons for compliance.[11]

To grant that government is needed as a co-ordinator but to deny that it needs to have a moral right to compliance with its decisions is to adopt an unsatisfactory, half-way position. For it is to grant that decisions must be made in the face of disagreement, but not to grant that they should be made by a decision-making procedure which normally yields decisions which create sufficient reasons for compliance with them. (The decisions of those with political authority create sufficient reason for compliance only normally, not always. For even if they create an exclusionary reason for compliance, they do not exclude, for example, great injustice of a decision from counting against compliance and overriding the reason for compliance.)

Notes

1. Replies to a few objections to consent theory can be found in Lewis (1940) and Tussman (1960). Brownsey (1978) replies most effectively to Hume's objections to contract and consent theory.

2. It is, of course, an argument for anarchism only in an unduly extended sense of this term. Anarchism, as a theoretical position, is the view that the state is, on balance, a harmful institution and should therefore be abolished and replaced with non-coercive, co-operative, social arrangements. Wolff argues only for the view that the state cannot have legitimate authority, not for the view that the state is a harmful institution. Indeed he leaves entirely open the possibility that the state is, on balance, useful, perhaps even necessary, for the promotion of human welfare. Simmons (1979) draws conclusions like Wolff's, since he also claims that political authority is an impossibility and leaves entirely open the possibility that the state is a worthwhile institution. He, too, accordingly, is misguided in labelling his position an anarchist one. Raz tries to save this use of the term 'anarchism'

122

by calling Wolff's position 'weak', as distinct from 'strong', anarchism. But the claim that the state ought to be abolished is so central to anarchism that any view which does not endorse this claim should not be called anarchism at all.

3. Wolff distinguishes between *de facto* and *de jure* authority and claims that only the latter involves a right to rule. It may be better not to speak of *de facto* authority, since to do so seems to involve a confusion of either power and authority-over or, possibly, of authority-with and authority-over. So Wolff's legitimate authority is here designated authority-over.

4. There is room for misunderstanding here. If it is inconvenient for me to clear out the storeroom at the time I'm ordered to do it, I can tell my superior that this is so and ask whether I can do it some other time. But, if, in the face of my request, the order is repeated, then it would be a mistake of practical reasoning to offer the inconvenience of following the order as a justification for not complying with it.

5. 'Unnecessary shuffle' is, of course, Rawls's not Hume's, phrase (1971, p. 32).

6. The above discussion of Hume's putative refutation of original contract or popular consent theory should make it clear that Kenneth R. Minogue misinterprets Hume when he writes that:

> Hume's famous essay on the subject attacked the contractarians for not answering the question that interested Hume (how did society in fact come into existence?) rather than the question which had interested them (how is sovereign power rightfully or rationally constructed?). (1978, pp. 133–4.)

In fact Hume wishes to refute both the view that there was an original contract and the view that (present) popular consent binds us to government.

7. It is assumed, in the next few paragraphs, that continued residence, say, when one ceases to be a political minor, counts as tacit consent, *provided* it is voluntary. This makes it possible to discuss the objection that it cannot be sufficiently free. The quite different objection that continued residence, even if free, is not sufficient to amount to tacit consent, is dealt with in the next chapter (see 'Some necessary reforms' and 'Political education').

8. Note 3 to Chapter 4 also applies to the present claim.

9. Readers who think this circumstance unreal are referred to the seven children of the Breton Nationalist couple M. and Mme. Manrot Le Goarnic (see the *Guardian*, 14 December 1974). The French government of the day refused to admit the existence of these children since they were given Breton first names, which was (at least at the time) contrary to French law. Hence they were not listed on government records, their parents were not able to claim social security allowances for them, they had no identity papers, and the eldest boy had been refused a driver's licence.

10. The contrast between voluntary and compulsory associations can be made with regard to at least two features of associations. Usually the contrast refers to membership in associations, but it can also refer to whether there are sanctions to non-compliance with the rules of an association by those who are members of it. The version of consent theory I defend is

committed to the claim that membership in an authoritative state must be voluntary, but not to the claim that laws must not have sanctions attached to them which are applied to those who break them.

11. I here follow Raz's statement of the co-ordination justification of political authority. (1975, p. 64.)

7

Reforms Required to Maximise Consent-based Political Obligation and Authority

Some necessary reforms

What reforms are necessary to realise consent-based obligation and authority to a greater extent than exists at present? The answer given here is far from exhaustive. Selected for discussion are a small number of reforms which clearly arise from what is written above and from the current literature on consent and political obligation. The reforms proposed are presented only sketchily.

According to the membership version of consent theory, consent consists in accepting membership in the state. In accepting such membership, one consents to the constitution (second-order laws), to governments which are appointed constitutionally and to (valid) first-order laws. What consent consists in and what one consents to, point to the two broad areas of political life in which reforms are necessary to make consent-based political obligation and authority more of a reality.

Let us begin with the consent which is involved in accepting membership in a state. The proportion of persons living within a state, who are under consent-based political obligation, will be maximised if:

(a) there is a legal right to emigrate and to change one's nationality;

(b) secession is constitutionally permitted if desired and feasible;

(c) a dissenters' territory is created.

Even in reasonably just states there will be people who wish to emigrate and others who may wish to secede.[1] If such people do not leave their present state (at least partly) because of sanctions attached to leaving, then their remaining in the state is coerced and they are not under political obligation. The three provisions

125

mentioned, for legal withdrawal from a state, must substantially reduce the proportion of citizens living there whose putative consent does not come off because they are coerced into membership. In the absence of such provisions, it is possible for most citizens to be coerced members.

Whether one is coerced into being a citizen does not depend on the mere existence of a threat of harm, but on whether one accepts citizenship *because* of the threat of harm. Unless citizens are legally free to leave their state, however, it will be extremely difficult to know what proportion of them freely accept membership.

We cannot know what proportion of East Germans would emigrate or secede were they legally free to do so. Any state concerned to show that its citizens are voluntary members, not captives, must at least make emigration and secession legal.

Express provisions for leaving the state are necessary to meet the objection that the consent of many citizens fails to come off because it is not sufficiently free. The following reform is necessary for the very possibility of native-born citizens consenting to obey the state through acceptance of full membership in it. For native-born citizens to be able to do this there has to be either a procedure by which they can, in accepting full membership, expressly consent to obey the state or a generally known convention to the effect that not leaving the state, when they cease to be political minors, counts as accepting full membership in it and as tacit consent to obey the state. I do not, at present, have a view as to which of these alternatives is preferable.) If consent is given tacitly, by means of the convention mentioned, then the convention must of course be one known to the person who is deemed to be tacitly consenting. Such knowledge in a community requires appropriate political education, a topic taken up later in this chapter (see 'Political education').

We may now turn to the issue of consent to the internal procedures of the state. The person who accepts membership in a state agrees to obey the first-order laws, its second-order (i.e. constitutional) law and constitutionally appointed governments. In doing so the citizen may seem to be faced with two problems which one may not expect to find together. The first is the take-it-or-leave-it-problem. Obviously, at the time when one accepts membership there is a constitution in existence and a government in office and there cannot be any possibility of an individual potential citizen making his acceptance of membership conditional on the constitution or the government being changed to conform to his preferences. He has to agree to obey the existing law and government or leave.

The citizen's second problem is that he may seem to be signing a blank cheque. The responsible exercise of the power to create agreement-based obligations requires that we have adequate knowledge of what it is we are agreeing to do. Yet in accepting membership in a state a person agrees to comply not only with present law and the present government but also with law that will in future be enacted and governments that will in future be (constitutionally) appointed. But since he is likely, in the modern state, to be only one of millions of citizens he has very little influence over the direction in which the law and politics of his state may change in future.

Both problems can be kept within tolerable bounds provided the state:

(a) has a written constitution;

(b) which guarantees citizens the right to participation in forming political policies;

(c) which guarantees citizens the right to participate in the selection of representative decision-makers;

(d) which guarantees citizens the right to stand for political office;

(e) which can be changed only by popular referendum;

(f) which includes a Bill of Rights setting legal limits to what first-order laws governments can enact and embodies a community consensus which indicates the moral limits on majority rule;

(g) which gives citizens the legal right to *initiate* changes in the constitution and first-order law.[2]

Inevitably, the typical modern citizen is one of many in his state and, unless he has above average political competence has only very limited influence on the political decisions which are made. But features (b), (c), (d) and (g) can guarantee that he has the legal right to attempt to bring about structural or policy changes in his state and can guarantee that he has such legal rights to the same extent as other citizens of his state.

Feature (g), one lacking in almost all existing states, may be especially useful to ensure that a popular desire for reform canot be blocked by a minority, especially that minority of citizens who are politically most active. For example, the SDP/Liberal Alliance advocates a change in the British electoral system from the present single-member constituency/first-past-the-post system to one of proportional representation. Now it is quite possible that a majority of British citizens should come to prefer proportional representation to the present system, but not so much as to vote in an Alliance government purely for the purpose of changing the electoral laws.

The Conservative and Labour parties could then frustrate a majority wish for reform (since such reform could reduce their power). The legal requirement to hold a referendum on any issue if, say, 5 per cent of the electorate petition for it, could circumvent such an attempt to block reform. This is especially so if there is a further legal requirement that the result of the referendum *must* be turned into law if it goes against the *status quo*. Hence, even if the prospective citizen must agree to obey an existing state holus-bolus at first, his exposure is less severe than might at first appear, in as far as he is guaranteed, *qua* citizen, a range of legal rights which later enable him to attempt to change the political form and policies of his state.

All the guarantees listed earlier from (a) through (g), help to make agreeing to obey the state unlike signing a blank cheque. But (a), (e), (f) and (g) do so most of all. For they limit what changes in political structure and policies governments can bring about. One of them, (g), also makes it possible to remove laws which a government insists on enacting but which, though constitutional, lack majority support.

The claim that the citizens of a state have a right of personal self-determination does not entail that the state of which they are citizens must have all the features listed. Nevertheless, each of the guarantees is appropriate for a state with citizens who have such a right. The more of these guarantees in a state, the more able are its citizens to exercise their right of self-determination. Needless to say, this is only so if these features exist, not just on paper, but in practice. Finally, it may be worth noting that, if a citizen's home state does change beyond recognition after he has accepted membership in it, he can always try to make use of his legal right to abandon his membership.

Political obligation and participatory democracy

The argument thus far assumes that representative democracy is consistent with the possibility of consent-based political obligation. It is the central claim, by contrast, of Carole Pateman's *The Problem of Political Obligation* (1979) that this is not so. She claims that the 'problem of political obligation can be solved only through the development of the theory . . . of participatory . . . democracy' (p. 1). It cannot be solved, she claims, within a liberal democratic theory. This is partly because the extent of economic inequality within the liberal democratic state permits an extent of political inequality which is inconsistent with the possibility of genuinely self-assumed political obligation and partly because liberal democracy is representative rather than participatory democracy. These objections to liberal democracy are independent of each other, since the social ownership or control of the means of production is theoretically and practically consistent both with representative and participatory political institutions at the national level. As noted, in the introductory paragraphs of Chapter 6, the socialist critique of liberal democracy lies beyond the scope of this book. However, it is important to consider whether Pateman is right in claiming that the problem of self-assumed obligation cannot be solved within liberal democratic theory, taken as a theory of representative (rather than participatory) democracy.

Pateman's central argument for this claim involves the following three steps.

(1) Liberal democratic theory is committed to a voluntarist theory of political obligation because of its assumption that people are naturally free and equal (1979, p. 12).

(2) But representative democracy involves an agreement to obey representative law-makers. And

(3) 'to agree to obey a few representatives . . . is to deny that individuals are free and equal' (1979, p. 151).

Clearly (3) is the claim Pateman has to establish to substantiate her thesis that the problem of political obligation cannot be solved within a theory of representative democracy. Support for (3) is given in a number of places in Pateman's book and in a number of different ways. Here are typical examples of what she asserts:

(I)n (liberal democratic) voting citizens choose representatives who will determine the content of their political obligation (1979, p. 83).

The essence of the liberal democratic social contract is that individuals ought to . . . enter an agreement to . . . obey representatives . . . to whom they have alienated their right to make political decisions (1979, p, 19).

Authorising representatives . . . seems necessarily to involve the subordination of the judgement of individuals to that of others (1979, p. 89).

A promise to obey is a very special kind of commitment which
puts the individual into a position of voluntary heteronomy
(1979, p. 151).

So Pateman argues that representative democracy 'contradicts the
liberal ideal of individual freedom and equality' (1979, p. 151)
because it creates representatives who determine the content of the
political obligation of citizens and requires citizens to alienate their
right to make political decisions, to subordinate their judgement
to that of representatives, and to place themselves in a position of
voluntary heteronomy.

It is quite clear that Pateman intends this argument to be a fatal
objection to any kind of representative democracy, not just to some
of the existing liberal democracies, for she claims quite unequivocally
and without qualification that 'the problem of political obligation
can be solved only through the . . . theory . . . of participatory
. . . democracy' (1979, p. 1). But it is not clear what kind of contradiction she believes to hold between representative political
institutions and the liberal ideals of individual freedom and equality. In fact, she does not show that there is either a logical or a normative contradiction between the advocacy of representative political
institutions at the national level and the endorsement of the ideals
of individual freedom and equality.

To see whether there is any kind of contradiction between these
claims, we have to understand what is included in the political
obligation which poses the problem which allegedly cannot be solved
within a theory of representtive democracy. Although Pateman
seems to raise this question in her book (p. 97. p. 172), she does
not answer it. It seems clear that political obligation within a
representative state would have to include (a) an obligation to obey
the constitution of the state (its second-order laws), (b) an obligation to obey constitutionally appointed governments and (c) an
obligation to obey valid first-order laws enacted by such governments. It is clear, in liberal representative democracies, that the legal
right to determine the constitution can and often does rest with the
citizens at large, that the legal right to determine governments rests
with citizens via universal adult franchise, and that the legal right
to enact or rescind first-order laws rests with elected governments.

Pateman's argument against representative democracy depends
on a remarkably narrow understanding of what counts as political
decision-making. It is only with regard to first-order law-making
that, in representative democracy, the legal right of decision-making

rests with representatives. By contrast, decisions about the content of the constitution of the state, and about who is to make up the legislative and executive, rest with the citizens at large. Although Pateman assumes otherwise, these latter decisions are just as political as the first-order legislative decisions made by governments.

Hence, in liberal representative democracies, it is not true that the right of political decision-making is necessarily 'alienated' to representatives or that representatives 'determine the content' of political obligation, or that citizens subordinate their political judgements to that of representatives. As far as these claims are true at all, they are true only of the legal right to make first-order law, a right which is indeed delegated to representatives. But even with regard to first-order law, Pateman's claims are misleading unless heavily qualified.

First, a liberal democratic government's legal right to make first-order law has to be exercised within the limits set by the constitution (which can include an entrenched Bill of Rights) and within the limits set by the wishes of the electorate. Second, the latter limit can be reinforced by making it legally mandatory to hold a referendum on any legal proposal called for by public petition. (The possibility of including such a provision in the Australian Constitution is discussed by John McMillan, Gareth Evans and Haddon Storey, 1983, pp. 257-9.) Such a reform would make the electorate's legal heteronomy regarding first-order laws a very limited one indeed. For it could legally require legislatures to enact any (constitutional) law which the majority of citizens want but the government does not and to rescind any law enacted by a legislature but not wanted by most citizens. (The former procedure exists in some American states, the latter in Switzerland. See Dahl, 1970, pp. 71-2.) Third, morally, the heteronomy involved in representative democracy, is only a partial one. For, morally, at least within consent theory, being under political obligation is only a reason for political obedience, not a conclusive reason. As will be shown in more detail in the next chapter, the political obligation to obey an unjust but valid first-order law can be overriden by its injustice, making it possible for citizens to exercise their autonomy and to disobey the unjust law.

Pateman exaggerates the extent to which political decision-making has to be transferred to representatives in (liberal) representative democracies. Still, within the limits noted, the legal right to make first-order law is transferred to representatives in such states. Pateman may wish to claim that even this limited voluntary heteronomy of citizens is inconsistent with the liberal ideals of individual freedom and equality.

Pateman does not make clear what kind of inconsistency she thinks is involved here — whether logical or, in some sense, normative. Nothing she writes in *The Problem of Political Obligation* amounts to an argument that there is a *logical* inconsistency in claiming both that individual freedom and equality are ideals and that some political decision-making can be delegated. Nor is it likely that a sound argument for this claim can be constructed. For, provided membership in the state is voluntary and all citizens have a right to take part in choosing and changing the constitution and the first-order law-makers, then delegating some political decision-making is logically on a par with delegating other kinds of decision-making. There does not, for example, seem to be any logical inconsistency between valuing individual freedom and equality and authorising a literary agent to sell one's manuscript to a publisher.

Whether there is some kind of *normative* inconsistency between valuing individual freedom and equality and permitting others to make important decisions for one depends on what else one values. If a writer values the activity of writing at least as much as freedom and equality, then it may not be the case that he ought not to authorise an agent to make publishing deals for him. For he may then maximise the things he values by spending more of his limited time writing, for the small cost of a minor reduction in his freedom and equality with others. In the political sphere too some reduction in liberty and freedom may be justified by the need to compromise in the pursuit of these values and others. Many people may prefer, in a morally legitimate way, to delegate some political decision-making to representatives, within the kinds of limits noted, to enable them to spend more time with their families and friends, at work, or on intellectual, artistic or leisure activities. But also, in the political sphere, some reduction in individual freedom and equality is necessary simply because, to misquote Oscar Wilde, participatory democracy takes too many evenings. It is clear that anyone who values individual freedom and equality should also value participation in political decision-making. It is also clear that, even given the other things people value, much more participation in group decision-making then prevalent at present, is appropriate — most of all in decision-making in the workplace. But any plausible case for participatory democracy must be made within something like Dahl's Chinese-boxes model of political decision-making (1970, Chapter 2). Pateman's case fails because she does not do this.

Most citizens are affected by decisions which are made: at their workplace, by their local government, perhaps by a regional government, and by their national government. Disarmament and international pollution control require more effective international decision-making than we have at present. Many people are members of voluntary associations such as political parties, trade unions, professional associations and parent-teacher associations. Direct democracy with actual majority participation within all of these organisations is literally impossible because of time constraints, no matter how rapidly communication technology develops. It also seems clear that a merely formal direct democracy in all of these organisations, which is exercised by largely self-selected small minorities, is not preferable to representative democracy.

One reason for this view, as Dahl notes (1970, p. 50), is that genuinely representative institutions are more likely to be representative of different views within the community on given issues than a self-selected minority which actually exercises the formal right of all to participate. To add another: presumably at least 50 per cent of the members of an association would have to participate in a vote for the vote to yield an outcome binding on its members. But even if communication technology developed so that it would be physically possible for people to do all the necessary voting, time constraints would make it impossible for most of this to be *informed* voting. Thus the introduction of direct democracy within all the associations mentioned would result either in very few changes to the *status quo* (because most decisions by vote would be invalid due to insufficient votes being cast), or in members being compelled to cast votes most of which would inevitably be uninformed.

In short, effective direct democracy is at best only possible within some of the associations necessary for the good life. Therefore, any plausible case for direct democracy at any particular decision-making level or within any particular association has to be a case which shows that it is more important here than elsewhere. Pateman's case for direct democracy fails because she faces so few of the issues that have to be dealt with in such a case. As the following quote shows, she is well aware that an adequate conception of the political requires a recognition that many associations are political:

> The view of political obligation as a horizontal relationship between citizens . . . is compatible only with a revised democratic conception, and it presupposes a non-statist

political community as a political association of a multiplicity
of political associations. The members of the community are
citizens in many political associations, which are bound
together through horizontal and multifaceted ties of self-
assumed political obligation. (1979, p. 174.)[3]

But Pateman does not consider whether participatory democracy
in *all* of these associations is possible, nor does she acknowledge the
obvious — namely that it is not. Therefore, she also does not consider in which of the associations conducive to the good life participatory democracy is most important. Nor does she consider whether
there is one correct answer to this question for all contemporary
societies in which the conditions for some kind of democracy exist.
Hence, even if she is right in claiming that those who value freedom
and equality must advocate participatory democracy at some levels
of political decision-making, she has not established that the national
level of decision-making is one of these. Therefore she has not shown
that the problem of (self-assumed) political obligation cannot be solved within a theory of representative democracy at the national level.
   Not only is her argument for this claim inconclusive, but there
is a fatal objection to it. Pateman has to claim that the problem of
(self-assumed) political obligation cannot be solved within a theory
of liberal representative democracy because the delegation of first-
order law-making to representatives is inconsistent with the liberal
ideals of individual freedom and equality. Since there is no reason
to think this inconsistency is a logical one, it may reasonably be
interpreted as a normative one, i.e. as the claim that people who
value freedom and equality, ought, morally speaking, not to delegate
first-order legislation to representatives, and that they should enact
such legislation instead through direct democracy. The fatal objection to this claim is that either such direct democracy would be a
total sham or it would result in the legislative fossilisation of society. We are, of course, considering direct democracy at the national
level. Grant that it is financially and technologically possible for
proposed national legislation to be debated through the print and
electronic media and to be voted on painlessly through the electronic media. Alternative legislative proposals and discussion papers
on a particular issue could be distributed through newsagents as
cheaply and as quickly as can daily newspapers. But it is not
reasonable to suppose that citizens can be expected to develop and
maintain informed opinions on the entire gamut of legislative issues,
such as nuclear energy, national superannuation schemes, sexual

and racial discrimination, the taxation system, and so on.

As a measure of the difficulty, consider that the government of even a relatively small country such as Australia (with a population of 15 million) still enacts about 170 laws per year! (In addition, each state government enacts scores of further laws every year.) There are things that could be said in defence of direct democracy at the national level. But in the end it seems clear that it either would not work or that the associated costs would be too high. If no law could be enacted without majority participation in the vote, then most of the votes would be uninformed, and thus direct democracy would be a sham. Alternatively, the rate of legislation would have to be reduced to something like one enactment a month. Supporters of direct democracy do not and should not love the *status quo* enough to find this acceptable.

Political education

Joseph Tussman's *Obligation and the Body Politic* (1960) puts forward a consent theory of political obligation. Tussman acknowledges that an 'act can only be properly taken as "consent" if it is done "knowingly".' By this he means that the person performing the act must understand that his action involves his acceptance of the obligations of membership. Tussman grants that 'many native "citizens" (in liberal democracies) have in no meaningful sense agreed to anything' and adds that such people 'are political child-brides who have a status they do not understand and which they have not acquired by their own consent'. He concludes that such '(n)on-consenting adult citizens are, in effect, like minors who are governed without their own consent'. This, he observes, 'is a failure of political education' (1960, pp. 36–7).

On the basis of these remarks, a number of writers attribute to Tussman the view that the child-brides are under political obligation without their consent. Thus Pitkin writes that:

> He takes it for granted that everyone . . . is obligated to obey
> . . . even the man who has never given government or obligation a single thought . . . The clods are obligated, Tussman says, like children. (1960, p. 997.) Cf. Pateman, (1979, p. 15) and Simmons (1979, p. 36).

But Tussman does *not* write that the political child-brides are under political obligation without their consent, merely that they are 'governed without their consent'. Nor does he write anything else that commits him to the view that the child-brides are under political obligation. Nor, finally, is it the case that he ignores the implications of the existence of these non-consenting political child-brides in liberal democracies. For one of the main themes of his book is the need for political education to reduce the proportion of such adults in liberal democracies.

But while Tussman does not say that the child-brides are under political obligation, he does not explicitly acknowledge that they are not. Yet this has to be done. In another place (1977, p. 270) I cast doubt on this conclusion by asking whether typical citizens of liberal democracies are negligent in not considering the significance of accepting full citizenship in their states when they legally come of age. They know that to accept membership in an association puts one under an obligation to obey the rules of the association and they probably have some awareness that the state is an association. Therefore, perhaps they should realise that, in accepting full membership in the state when they come of age, they put themselves under an obligation to obey the state. If they do not realise this, they are perhaps negligent and negligent lack of awareness does not necessarily defeat the claim that one's action puts one under an obligation to do certain things.

Even if this argument is sound, it provides far too fragile a defence for a consent theory of political obligation and authority, given that the proportion of citizens it is likely to apply to in present liberal democracies may well be the majority. Only the most complacent adherents of an elitist theory of democracy could be satisfied with such a defence. Anyone else would wish to consider how to turn these political child-brides into politically aware citizens who have the opportunity knowingly to consent or not. As noted earlier, this requires either the introduction of an explicit acceptance-of-membership ceremony or the development of a generally known convention that remaining within the borders of a state, when one legally comes of age, normally counts as accepting full membership and as placing oneself under political obligation and authority. This in turn requires the introduction of a kind of political education not available now in any of the liberal democracies.

Unlike some other political systems, democracy requires for its effective operation politically educated citizens. Such citizens have to have some general understanding of the functions of a democratic state, of what makes political decision-procedures democratic, of the proper relationship between a democratic state and its citizens, and not only of the obligations of citizens in a democratic state but also of the rights and legal opportunities of such citizens. But if the present version of consent theory is at least roughly correct, then a fairly specific understanding of some political procedures is a necessary condition for the citizens of democracies to be under political obligation and for their states to have political authority over them. It is therefore essential that political education provide this.

The most important elements in the political education to be communicated are (a) that as far as membership is concerned the democratic state is a voluntary association, (b) that the ultimate right of political decision making rests with all the adult members of the state, (c) that in remaining within a state when one legally comes of age one accepts full membership in the state and thereby expressly or tacitly places oneself under political obligation and authority, (d) that in taking part in referenda or elections one places oneself under an obligation to accept their outcome whether one votes for or against the outcome determined by the vote, (e) that the obligations mentioned in (c) and (d) can be overridden by other moral considerations.

Such an understanding must be given to citizens within a general preparation for the choice they must make when they assume the normal rights of adult citizens, viz. whether to accept membership in the state in which they have grown up. This requires that they acquire an understanding of the admittedly often limited alternatives to such acceptance and some understanding of political systems other than their own, and political theories other than democratic theory. To provide this understanding is a task schools would have to tackle for all students not only those who aim for the highest level of secondary schooling.

Consent theory occupies a special, possibly even a unique, position among theories of political obligation and authority. A divine-right-of-kings theory of political obligation, for example, need not claim that the general acceptance of the theory is a necessary condition for the existence of political authority or political obligation. If political authority was indeed bestowed on Henry VIII directly by God, then logically his authority did not depend on most Englishmen accepting the divine-right theory. By contrast, consent theory presupposes that political authority can exist only to the extent to which citizens understand and accept that certain acts of consent create political authority. If they do not believe this then no acts of theirs can count as consent and without consent there is no political authority. Some may think that this reduces consent theory to absurdity. But if human beings do have the right of personal self-determination attributed to them by consent theory, then it cannot be absurd to conclude that a recognition of this right and its consent implications for authority-over relations among adults is a pre-condition for the creation of such authority relations.

Notes

1. In case the latter claim is not obviously true, consider the Kurds whose contiguous territory is divided among Turkey, Syria, Iran, Iraq and the Soviet Union. This ancient nation cannot achieve national self-determination except through the creation of an independent Kurdish state, no matter how internally just their present host states are. I speak of national self-determination in the illustration just used. But are not nationalism and consent theory incompatible, the former being a collectivist doctrine, the latter an individualist one? There are of course versions of nationalism which are incompatible with consent theory, but the assertion of a right to national self-determination is not. Individuals have a right to personal self-determination. Therefore, groups have a right to group self-determination, along the lines developed in Chapter 3 (see 'Consent theory and secession'). Therefore, groups which are nations have a right to national self-determination. This, of course, is a right which the members of a nation may be able to exercise in ways other than by being an independent state and which the members of the nation may not be able to exercise at all, if they are members of different states and do not want to set up an independent nation-state or cannot agree on what sort of independent nation-state to form.

2. This list of features of a state which would keep the two problems posed within tolerable bounds is not meant to be exhaustive. The features are representative of those which can minimise the two problems.

3. Pateman does not explain how she can consistently use an excessively narrow concept of the political in her most important objection to representative democracy (see above, this chapter) and a very wide concept in her advocacy of direct democracy.

8

Political Obligation and Moral Ought

('Ought' is here used in the sense of 'conclusive reason', introduced in Chapter 2.)

This chapter explores the relationship, within consent theory, between the statements

P is under political obligation to do X and

P morally ought to do X (where X is an act P's government requires him to perform).

In 'Obligation but not ought' cases are explored where P is under political obligation to obey a certain law but it is not the case that he ought to obey it or even the case that he ought not to obey it. In 'Ought but not obligation' cases are explored where P is not under political obligation but it is the case that he ought to obey. This is followed by a discussion of the relationship between political obligation and political legitimacy in 'Political legitimacy' and between political obligation and the responsibilities of citizenship in 'Different senses of political obligation'.

Obligation but not ought

We must distinguish between cases in which an agent does not claim that his law-breaking is morally justified (e.g. the ordinary burglar stealing for personal gain) and cases in which he does claim moral justification (e.g. civil disobedience). In the latter case, a further distinction can be made between citizens who reject the claim that they are under political obligation (e.g. revolutionary dissent) and citizens who do not reject the claim that they are under political obligation, but claim moral justification for breaking a particular

139

law (morally justified selective disobedience). The following discussion deals only with the last type of case.

It is clear that there must be some scope, within consent theory, for morally justified disobedience of law which one is under political obligation to obey. For according to consent theory this obligation (and the correlative political authority of the state) is created by an agreement to obey; and an agreement to do something creates a defeasible, not an indefeasible, reason for action. Admittedly this reason is an exclusionary one, but exclusionary reasons are not necessarily indefeasible reasons. (See Chapter 2.) In promising to do X one creates a reason for doing X which commits one to exclude certain kinds of reasons from consideration when one comes to assessing whether one ought to do X. These include mere personal inconveniences and mere utility. But they do not include *all* other considerations.

If G has promised to meet R at time *t*, then the consideration that it is inconvenient for G to go to the meeting, or that G may produce a little more happiness by spending time with another person, will not count as a valid reason against meeting R. But if G is the only person who can take his seriously sick son to hospital, then G does have a reason, which is not excluded from consideration whether G ought to keep his promise, and which at least in some cases would override the promissory obligation. The same kinds of judgements apply to consent-based political obligation. That one has agreed to obey the law creates a moral reason for obeying the law which excludes certain kinds of reasons from counting against obeying the law. But it does not exclude from consideration all moral reasons for disobeying the law. Hence, there is some scope, within consent theory, for morally justified disobedience.

One can be justified in breaking bad law either 'privately', or publicly. The severe legal restrictions on the sale of contraceptives in the Republic of Ireland unjustifiably impose the religious-moral-metaphysical beliefs of some on the conduct of others. The effect of this ban on the lives of many people can be so grave that it seems plausible that the public breaking of this law with the aim of drawing attention to its badness and of having it repealed (i.e. civil disobedience) can be justified. But it also seems clear that not all justified disobedience of this law needs to be such civil disobedience. People who need such contraceptives can be quite justified in disobeying the law 'in private', i.e. without drawing attention to their doing so and without any intention to bring the law into disrepute by breaking it.

There are some bad laws which one cannot readily break by way of public protest against them, e.g. a law which forbids suicide and under which people who unsuccessfully attempt suicide can be prosecuted. In such cases, justified civil disobedience may involve breaking laws which one does not consider evil as such. For example, people may disrupt court proceedings against unsuccessful suicides thereby breaking laws governing court proceedings which are not deemed bad as such.

The following seem to be plausible examples of justifiable disobedience of good law:

(a) in order to reach a dying spouse in time one breaks some traffic laws;

(b) in order to stop one's children from starving to death, one steals from the rich;

(c) in order to avoid long-term imprisonment for a crime of which one has wrongly been found guilty by due legal process, one escapes from prison.

Phillip Arantz's 'whistle-blowing' seems a very plausible example of a further type of justified disobedience: breaking a law where this is a particularly effective way of drawing attention to the law-breaking of others. In 1971, Arantz, an employee in the crime statistics section of the New South Wales police department, broke the regulation which forbids such employees making public statements about departmental affairs, by revealing to the press that the police department was deliberately overstating its crime-solving rate by up to 70 per cent in its public statements. He did so only after he had repeatedly drawn the deception to the attention of his superiors without the practice being stopped.[1]

In the types of cases presented, disobedience of the law can be morally justified. Obviously this assumes that the reasons for breaking the law, in such cases, override the reasons for obeying it, including the reason involved in being under political obligation. Some of these reasons for breaking a law can be natural obligations to break it and some can perhaps be institutional obligations. If a law, while being valid, is also grossly unjust, and if there is an obligation not to act in a grossly unjust way, some people may be under a natural obligation to break this law.

Can there also be an institutional obligation to break a law which one is under promise-based political obligation to obey? The answer is probably affirmative but, in the absence of a fully developed theory of promising, it is difficult to be certain. The most important and most likely candidate for such an obligation to disobey arises out of agreements of groups of people who are working to change the law, partly through civil disobedience. Michael Walzer has noted that when it comes to disobeying the law, the 'heroic encounter between sovereign individual and sovereign state', is 'terrifyingly unequal'. What sustains civil disobedience, is not the 'mere individual right to rebel' but 'the mutual undertakings' of a group of citizens dedicated to the abolition of an unjust law (1970, p. 22). Normally, only group activity sustained over a considerable period of time has any chance to bring about a change in the law. Such activity requires solidarity which in turn is helped by members of the group undertaking to collectively engage in the struggle against some law(s).

It seems plausible to conclude that such mutual undertakings can come off, even though they involve citizens giving an undertaking to break a law that they are already under a promissory, political obligation to obey. One reservation to be noted, however, is that a promise to do X does not come off if the very purpose of making it is to create a moral reason for breaking a previous promise not to do X. There remain other circumstances in which it seems plausible that two conflicting promises can come off. Perhaps this is especially so, if the two promises are temporally remote from each other and involve *types* of actions which may, but need not, involve *particular* actions which cannot both be done. The notorious Von Bulow trials provide an illustration. During the second trial of Von Bulow for attempting to murder his wife (the verdict of the first trial was overturned by a higher court), Mrs Von Bulow's maid

> . . . acknowledged that she had twice lied under oath in the first trial, saying that she did so because she had promised Mrs Von Bulow that she would tell neither about her mistress's facelift nor her desire to divorce Von Bulow.[2]

The political case, while not quite analogous, seems to be sufficiently like the case just mentioned to make it plausible that one can be both under promise-based political obligation to obey a particular law and under a promissory obligation to one's fellow activists to break it. (In other words the existence of the first promise may not prevent the second promise from coming off.)

To accept membership in a state is to agree to obey its laws. It seems unrealistic to assume that a state can accept anything other than an agreement to obey every law, including those to be enacted validly during the future membership of the citizen. This body of law need not *necessarily* include laws so morally bad as to justify civil disobedience. But our knowledge of contemporary liberal democracies makes it likely that there will be bad law. Moreover, unjust laws can be passed after the initial agreement to obey all laws. Equally, unjust laws, even if in existence at the time of the initial agreement to obey, may not have been laws of which the citizen was aware. Given the enormous body of legislation in contemporary liberal democratic states, even the most conscientious and responsible of potential citizens cannot reasonably be expected to check whether all existing laws are morally sufficiently acceptable for him to promise to obey them. Admittedly, this makes an agreement to obey the law more like signing a blank cheque than desirable, but (as shown in Chapter 7) not so much as to undermine consent theory. Hence, if some time after agreeing to obey the law, a citizen finds himself confronted with a morally iniquitous law whose repeal requires group action, it seems plausible that such a citizen's promise to engage in civil disobedience can come off and create an obligation to break a law which he is already under promise-based political obligation to obey.

In summary, consent theory must allow some scope for morally justified disobedience of laws which one is under political obligation to obey. The moral reasons for disobedience can include natural obligations and, probably, also, institutional obligations to disobey. It would be helpful to be able to add to this a theory on the weighting or ordering of moral reasons for action so as to make it easier to say when the balance of conflicting reasons dictates compliance or non-compliance with the law. Such a theory would be especially helpful since, at least within the theory of justified political obedience presented here, citizens are confronted with quite complex problems of moral reasoning. For example, a person who has accepted membership in a state and voted in the last election has two promissory obligations to obey the law, his political obligation arising out of accepting membership in the state and his obligation to accept the outcome of the voting procedure in which he took part. If, subsequent to these acts, the government (validly) enacts a grossly unjust law, and the citizen enters mutual undertakings with others to break it in acts of civil disobedience, he also has a natural obligation and an institutional obligation to break the law. In addition there *may* be other moral reasons for or against obeying the law and some of the reasons stated are exclusionary reasons. Unfortunately, no generally accepted theory as yet exists on the weighting of moral reasons for action, and this is not an appropriate place at which to attempt to make good the lack. At this stage, accordingly, the reader must be left to supply his own general theory.

Ought but not obligation

The claim 'If a government does not have authority to govern, then it cannot be morally justified in exercising power' is theoretically convenient and simple — but also false. If people have a right of self-determination, then governments cannot have political authority without the consent of the governed. Nevertheless, governments may be morally justified in exercising power without consent. According to consent theory, the consent of the governed is a necessary condition of political authority and obligation. If there is no such consent, there is no political authority or obligation. But since institutional morality is only part of morality, there *could* be other moral considerations which justify the exercise of power by a non-authoritative regime and which morally require obedience of those governed.

Consider a non-political case. Jack Daniels who knows that he gets violent after he has had a few drinks too many, asks Sean O'Casey, his less volatile drinking companion, to restrain him whenever this happens. Hence O'Casey has the (institutional) right to restrain Daniels whenever the latter gets violent. But even if O'Casey did not have this right and did not even know Daniels he might still be morally justified in restraining him if he got violent. There are reasons of natural morality which may be sufficient to justify restraining a violent person; if, in addition, one has an institutional right to do so, then one may be doubly justified in doing so.

A few examples may help to make plausible an analogous claim in the political sphere. If an East German is coerced into staying in East Germany, then he is not under political obligation and, especially, he has no obligation to remain in East Germany. However, if the government will carry out severe reprisals against his relatives should he escape, then it may well be the case that, morally speaking, he ought not to leave East Germany.

According to the account of political authority given in this book, if a minority in a state are prevented by force from seceding, then the government of that state ceases to be the authoritative government of the group that wishes to secede. However, assume the region wishes to secede solely to maintain an existing system of slavery. Then the government may well be morally justified in preventing secession by force until the slaves are emancipated, although in doing so it ceases to be the authoritative government of the group that wishes to secede.

It may be clear to the army in a state that the creation of a military dictatorship is the only feasible way of preventing an impending civil war which would decimate the population and virtually destroy the nation. If the army assumes the office of government by force and against the wishes of the majority of the people, it would not have political authority and the people would not be under political obligation. But, plausibly, if the dictators acted in the interests of the people they would be morally justified in assuming power and the people ought to obey them.

A non-authoritative government can be morally justified in governing and considerations of natural morality can be sufficient to justify the exercise of political power in the absence of political authority and obligation. It in no way follows from this that political philosophy should abandon its concern with political obligation and authority as superficial, to concern itself instead with the specification of the conditions of natural morality which government must satisfy to be morally justified. For it is only in abnormal circumstances that a government which lacks political authority can be morally justified in exercising power over people, just as it is only in abnormal circumstances that one adult is morally justified in controlling the actions of another sane adult without an institutional right to do so. Where no such abnormal circumstances hold, there is no moral justification for the exercise of political power by some people over others, unless there is a political authority relationship between them.

What makes circumstances abnormal? The presence of conditions which prevent people from exercising their capacity of self-determination successfully. Two importantly different types of such conditions have already been alluded to. First, people may have the capacity for self-determination, but it may not have been developed into an operative ability. (They may be as Mozart would have been without musical education.) Marxism may be interpreted as claiming this about a proletariat which suffers from false consciousness and is in the grip of socio-political theories which are ideological in the Marxist sense (i.e. in the grip of theories about the state which are largely false but whose general acceptance is in the interests of the ruling class). In the second type of condition, people do have an operative ability, not just a capacity or potential

145

for self-determination, but circumstances external to them prevent them from exercising the ability successfully. Perhaps total war (especially nuclear) provides an example.

Political obligation (the obligation of obedience which arises out of one's acceptance of membership in the state) is only one possible reason among others for obeying a particular state. But it has a special place among possible reasons for political obedience. For, to use a medical metaphor, it is essential to, and figures prominently in, a theory of the 'healthy' state, i.e. a state in which there exists an authority relation between the state and its citizens. On the other hand, that part of the theory of political obedience which deals with situations where the reasons for obedience do not include consent-based reasons, belongs to the theory of the 'pathology' of the state.

Political legitimacy

Political authority consists in a moral right to make decisions which are binding on others, a right which one has by virtue of a role within a hierarchically organised group. Political obligation is a moral obligation to comply with the decisions of those who have political authority. Hence political obligation and political authority are correlatives: one logically cannot exist without the other.

Within consent theory it is possible for a government to have political authority over some of the persons living in the territory under its jurisdiction but not over others. As already suggested, a government can be said to be authoritative if it has political authority over at least the majority in the territory under its jurisdiction. In other words, it is an authoritative government if at least more than half the people in its territory are under political obligation.

The question now to be raised concerns the logical relationship between a government being authoritative and its being legitimate. Obviously this relationship must depend on the criteria used for ascribing political legitimacy to governments. At least three kinds of criteria can be distinguished (cf. Simmons, 1979, pp. 40–1, pp. 195–200).

(1) A government can be called legitimate on procedural grounds, i.e. because it has acquired power in the proper way (constitutionally), regardless of its substantive merits.

(2) Or it can be called legitimate on substantive grounds, i.e. because it pursues good ends and uses good means, regardless of

146

whether it has come to power in the proper way.

(3) From these internal criteria of legitimacy we can distinguish an external criterion, viz. whether a government is recognised as legitimate by other governments. Such international recognition of legitimacy can be based on the procedural or the substantive criterion already mentioned. Or it can be based on a government having effective control over most of the territory and population of the state over which it claims jurisdiction (even if it satisfies neither the procedural nor the substantive criterion for legitimacy). Of course, governments are often called legitimate because they satisfy some combination of the three criteria of legitimacy.

The relationship between external legitimacy and authoritativeness is one of indifference. A government can have external legitimacy without being authoritative (having majority consent) and vice versa. The same relationship holds between a government having internal legitimacy on substantive grounds and being authoritative. A government can have majority consent even if it does not rate very highly on substantive normative grounds. Earlier in this chapter (see 'Ought but not obligation') it was claimed that, under conditions which make it impossible for citizens to exercise their capacity for self-determination, a government may be justified in exercising political power without consent. Such a government could have substantive legitimacy without being authoritative. The relationship between a government being authoritative and having procedural legitimacy is stronger: the former implies the latter, but not vice versa. If a government is authoritative then it also has procedural legitimacy. For consent consists in accepting membership in the state, and in accepting such membership one agrees, *inter alia*, to obey the constitution and constitutionally appointed governments. But governments can have procedural legitimacy without being authoritative, since the procedures (the constitution etc.) may not have majority consent. Thus, within consent theory, an authoritative government is not necessarily a legitimate one, and a legitimate government is not necessarily an authoritative one. In any critical discussion of consent theory these terms cannot be used interchangeably.

Different senses of political obligation

Throughout this discussion of consent theory, 'political obligation' is used in a narrow sense. That is, it refers to the obligation to obey the state which is the correlative of political authority. Johnson objects to this narrow sense on the ground that, in accepting membership in a state, one accepts more than an obligation to obey it. Johnson proposes to have the term refer to an obligation to care for the common good of the community (1975, p. 26). This objection involves a substantive and a terminological claim.

The discussion set out earlier in this book reveals no disagreement with Johnson's substantive claim. Consent is identified with accepting membership in the state and is claimed, therefore, to provide the basis of an obligation to obey the state — political obligation in the narrow sense. But this equation of consent with acceptance of membership in the state is quite consistent with the further claim that membership in the state, i.e. citizenship, requires much more than a mere obligation to obey. The arguments presented above at least suggest that membership also involves a requirement, as far as possible for given individuals to participate in the political affairs of society, to assume political office, to improve social life through political means, to break laws where necessary and to join with others in campaigns to remove unjust policies, laws or institutions. The only difference between the narrow sense of political obligation used here and the wider sense advocated by Johnson is purely terminological.

In a wide sense of 'political obligation', one may well say that the obligations of citizenship include most or all of the activities mentioned in the previous paragraph. But this wide sense can easily be distinguished from the narrow sense. Critics of consent theory have often written as if the theory tried to explain political obligation in the wide sense in terms of consent. But no consent theorist has done so. Hence, to avoid any possibility of the narrow scope of consent theory being overlooked or misunderstood, it is best to continue to use 'political obligation' in the narrow sense in which consent theorists have always used it.

Notes

1. Justified whistle-blowing indeed! Arantz was dismissed from the police force in 1972 for breaking departmental regulations. After a 13-year campaign for reinstatement, he accepted an offer in 1985 of 250,000 dollars from the New South Wales Government in compensation for his treatment by the police department. (The *Sydney Morning Herald*, 26 March 1985 and David Hickie, 1985, pp. 270–3.)

2. The *Sydney Morning Herald*, 1 May, 1985.

9

Summary of the Membership Version of Consent Theory

Summary

The state is not a naturally occurring phenomenon which is beyond human control. Much of what we find in the state is the outcome of luck and chance. Much is the unintended result of the interaction of many. But much is also the intended result of human decisions. And any given institution can be reformed or overthrown by human effort. Normal adults have capabilities which entitle them to a say in the decisions that determine their political relationships. Therefore, minorities have no right to coerce or deceive majorities into political arrangements the latter do not want. And majorities have no right to prevent individuals from emigrating, or territorially concentrated minorities from seceding. With regard to membership, the liberal democratic state must be, as far as possible, a voluntary association. Being born into a particular state should not make us the captives of this state.

Such is the spirit, in brief, which animates this book. The exposition of the version of consent theory presented here is spread over the previous chapters. It is, therefore, appropriate to attempt a summary of it. The central claim is that, within liberal democratic theory, actual personal consent must be the basis of political obligation and authority. Political authority is understood as authority-over, involving a moral, not merely a legal, right to make decisions which are binding on those under authority. Political obligation is understood as that particular moral obligation which is the correlative of political authority. In this narrow sense of political obligation, it has to be distinguished from other reasons, including other obligations, to comply with the state. Liberal democratic theory claims that the state is necessary for the promotion of liberty, justice and human welfare and that political authority is, therefore, justified. It also assumes that people are capable of and, therefore, have a right to personal self-determination. It is, therefore, committed to the claim that the basis of political authority (and political obligation) must be the actual personal consent of those under political authority.

Consent consists in accepting membership in the state. In doing so one agrees to obey the state and, therefore, puts oneself under its authority and under an obligation to comply with it. Because political authority and political obligation are consent-based, they constitute only a reason, not a conclusive reason, for obeying the state. Admittedly the reason is an exclusionary one, but it is, nevertheless, defeasible because it does not exclude all possible reasons against obedience from counting. (Hence what we may call the narrow scope of consent theory: consent does not try to explain every possible reason for complying with the state.) In consenting, one agrees to obey first-order laws, second-order laws and constitutionally appointed governments. Regarding both types of laws, the obligation is wholistic, it is an obligation to comply with all the laws which apply to a particular person. Fulfilment of political obligation is owed to the state, since it is the correlative of political authority and it is the state which has this authority with its right to compliance with authoritative determinations.

Consent theory distinguishes between political authority and obligation on the one hand and political legitimacy on the other. It does not claim that governments which have procedural or substantive or external legitimacy must be based on consent.

If people have a right of personal self-determination then their political relationships must be voluntary. This means that the continuing unity of the state must also be voluntary. Therefore, liberal democratic theory is committed, not only to individuals being allowed to abandon membership of the state, but also the permissibility of secession by territorially concentrated groups, as far as possible.

Naturalised citizens can consent expressly when they accept citizenship. Native-born citizens can also consent expressly if an appropriate procedure is introduced; or they can consent tacitly by continuing to live in their native state when they cease to be political minors, provided there is a convention to this effect. The alternatives to accepting membership in the state into which one is born are emigration, secession, movement to a dissenters' territory (if such is created) or, if one cannot or does not want to leave one's state, a public refusal to accept membership.

Acceptance of membership in the state puts one under political obligation and authority. The right of personal self-determination which requires that political obligation and authority be consent-based, also requires that political decision-making in the state be democratic. In large representative democracies this is most likely to involve elections of governments and occasional referenda on legislative proposals. Voting in such elections and referenda, if fair and effective, creates additional self-assumed obligations to obey the government and some laws. A further self-assumed obligation to obey some laws is created by accepting the benefits of the law-abidingness of one's fellow citizens.

The consent which creates political obligation and authority is identified with accepting membership in the state because only this consent can explain all parts of political obligation and its wholistic extent. The consent which creates political obligation has to explain an obligation to obey all first- and second-order law and the political authority of the state. Voting in democratic elections cannot account for the political obligation of election abstainers and of those who are prevented from voting by misadventure, nor can it account for the political obligation to obey second-order law. The acceptance of the benefits of the law-abidingness of one's fellow citizens cannot account for the political obligation to obey all types of first-order laws, nor for political authority.

In addition to self-assumed obligations to obey the state, there is a natural obligation to obey it as far as it promotes liberty, justice and human welfare.

An account of justified political obedience in terms of natural obligation is not adequate, because often there is disagreement among citizens as to whether there is a natural obligation to obey a particular law. This difficulty can be alleviated by the creation of political authority, i.e. authority which involves a moral right to compliance with its decisions. For such decisions can create a reason for compliance with the law which is independent of the substantive merits of the law and which can be sufficient for compliance with it for those who are uncertain about its substantive merits.

The natural obligation to obey the state arising out of its usefulness, and the self-assumed obligations to obey it arising out of accepting membership, are not alternative, mutually exclusive accounts of justified political obedience. Rather, they are equally necessary, complementary parts of it. The state's usefulness explains why political authority is justified, consent why a particular state can rightfully claim a particular person as a member and why some

151

particular individuals have a right to occupy the office which carries political authority.

Citizens of (nearly) just states have natural and institutional obligations to obey the state. These obligations are defeasible reasons for obeying the state. Therefore, citizens can be morally justified in breaking some laws, even of a nearly just state. This can be so either *because* a particular law is *unjust* or *in spite of* it being *just*. In the former case (unjust law) the consent obligation can be overridden by the injustice of the law. In the latter case (just law) the obligation(s) to obey it can be overridden by even weightier obligations to do something which requires breaking the just law.

The main focus in this book is on political obligation and authority. The account supplied is only a fragment, though an important one, of a theory of justified political obedience. Some other elements of such a theory are sketched in so as to make the consent theory of political obligation and authority plausible. Hence it is noted that, in addition to political obligation, citizens can have other institutional and natural obligations to obey the state. They can also have moral reasons, including natural and, perhaps, institutional obligations, to disobey the state.

These features of the theory of justified political obedience have two important consequences. First, in some cases it may be a difficult task of practical reasoning to determine whether, morally speaking, one ought to obey a particular law. Second, the balance of reasons for and against obeying the state will differ among citizens. One citizen may have a number of obligations to obey a particular law and no reason for disobeying it, another may have only the political obligation to obey it and moral reasons for disobeying it which override this obligation. These consequences of the theory reflect its merits, since they adequately capture our pre-theoretical view of the complexity of moral reasoning in the political realm.

Any theory of justified political obedience which recognises both natural and consent-based reasons for complying with the state has to recognise the potential tension between these types of reasons. A regime which may be morally justified in exercising political power may not have the consent of citizens and citizens may consent to a regime they ought not to consent to. Liberal democratic theory assumes that this tension is normally only a potential one, because it assumes that citizens are normally sufficiently rational and sufficiently informed to consent to regimes that deserve such consent and not to consent to regimes that do not.

This book omits any attempt to assess the extent to which citizens of existing liberal democracies can plausibly be claimed to consent to obey the state by knowingly accepting membership in it. The aim, rather, is to make plausible the claim that, *in theory*, only consent-based political obligation and authority is consistent with liberal democratic assumptions about human nature. Hence the development and defence of a reform, not a *status quo*, version of consent theory. Whatever the extent of political obligation and authority in existing liberal democracies, it would be substantially increased if secession became more permissible, dissenters' territories were established, all citizens educated to understand that authoritative political ties must be voluntary, and a convention established to the effect that continued residence in a state, when one ceases to be a political minor, counts as tacit political consent.

Even in nearly just states there may be some residents who are not under political obligation or authority. In the last few chapters, a number of types of cases which may fall into this category are identified. There may be some who refuse to consent, but who are not expelled. There may be some who wish to leave, but are not allowed to, because (as minors) they took on special responsibilities which they are now trying to escape. And there may be some whose putative consent is coerced and, therefore, does not come off. (They may wish to, but cannot, leave and consent only to avoid sanctions attached to a refusal to agree to obey.) However, in a reasonably just state, only a small minority will be in such a position and it is not a condition of the adequacy of the theory of political obligation and authority that it account for a strictly universal authority relation between the state and all its residents. This book claims (i) that, within liberal democratic theory, consent must be the basis of political authority and obligation (ii) that such consent-based political authority and obligation is possible without utopian changes to existing liberal democracies. The second of these claims is substantiated provided a very large majority of persons living in a state can be under such self-assumed obligation and authority. (Here an authoritative state is understood to be one which has political authority over at least the majority of its adult citizens.) In a (nearly) just state those who are *not* under political obligation would still have other moral reasons for obeying most laws.

Consent or contract?

The theory of political obligation advanced here is stated in terms of consent rather than contract. Pateman, following an unpublished paper by Gordon Schochet, claims that 'consent theory' and 'social contract theory' should not be treated as interchangeable labels (1979, p. 22). She distinguishes between them in this way: *Social contract* explains how (in the beginning) free and equal individuals can join together in a political community and put themselves under political authority; *Consent* has to be added to explain how those who are born into the state created by the original contractors come in turn to be under the political authority of this state.

If this distinction between consent and contract is correct, then it is right to express the theory advanced here in terms of consent. For the days of the state of nature are well past and most of us now belong to the generations subsequent to those of the founding fathers. But is this distinction between consent and contract theory entirely adequate? Apart from one major qualification, it probably is. For present purposes, contract is best understood as a mutual promise (If you promise to do X , I promise to do Y) so that it can be distinguished from a (unilateral) promise (I promise to do X — you do not have to promise to do anything). It seems that, within the voluntaristic approach to political obligation and authority adopted in this book, the voluntary acts of commitment which create political obligation and authority are an accumulation of individual (unilateral) promises (or agreements or consents) rather than society-wide mutual promises or mutual promises between the state and individual citizens.

The exception to this is the possibility, mooted in Chapter 7, of express consent given by native-born citizens in an acceptance-of-full-membership ceremony, when they assume full political rights. For if such a procedure were devised it should be of a contractual form, with the state agreeing to extend the rights and privileges of citizenship to the person assuming full membership and this person agreeing to comply with the law of the state. (That there is much more to citizenship than this mutual agreement does not invalidate the point being made.)

In the absence of a procedure for express consent, it seems most realistic to understand political obligation and authority as involving consent rather than contract. Consider an established state going on over time. For the sake of illustration, let it be a reasonably just democracy in which representative legislators are elected to office and other officials are appointed. Let there be a generally known convention that continuing to live in the state into which one is born, when one is legally entitled to assume full political rights, counts as tacit consent to comply with the law. Here citizens, as subjects of the state, consent to comply with the law by continuing to live in the state, by voting in elections and by accepting the benefits of their fellow citizens' law-abidingness. Moreover, many citizens as political office-holders (as representatives in the legislature, as ministers in the government, as judges etc.) agree to carry out the duties of their offices according to the law. It seems that at least most of these acts of consent are not parts of social or political contracts.

Next, consider the creation of a new state by secession as the result of a series of referenda in which a group votes for secession and for a new constitution. Again what we seem to have here is a great number of individuals voting and thereby implicitly agreeing to be bound by the results of referenda. We do not seem to have any mutual agreements between citizens or between citizens and the new state.

Hence, apart from states with procedures for express consent, the language of consent rather than contract seems appropriate for referring to the voluntary acts which are the basis of political obligation and authority and of the additional, freely created obligations to comply with the law that have been mentioned. The political authority relation between the state and its citizens and such other obligations as may exist are not the product of either a society-wide contract or an accumulation of bilateral contracts between the state and individual citizens, but the product of an agglomeration of unilateral acts of consent.

Bibliography

Arendt, H. (1954) 'What is Authority?' in *Between Past and Future. Six Exercises in Political Thought*, Viking Press, New York.

Armstrong, D.M. (1973) *Belief Truth and Knowledge*, Cambridge University Press, Cambridge.

Austin, J.L (1965) *How To Do Things With Words*, Clarendon Press, Oxford.

—— (1964) *Sense and Sensibilia*, Clarendon Press, Oxford.

Bachrach, Peter and Baratz, Morton S. (1974) *Power and Poverty*, Oxford University Press, New York.

Bates, S. (1972) 'Authority and Autonomy', *The Journal of Philosophy*, 69, pp. 175-9.

Bell, David, R. (1971) 'Authority', in *The Proper Study*: Royal Institute of Philosophy Lectures 1969-1970, Macmillan, London, pp. 190-203.

Bell, David V.J. (1975) *Power, Influence and Authority*, Oxford University Press, New York.

Benn, S.I. and Peters, R.S. (1969) *Social Principles and the Democratic State*, George Allen and Unwin, London.

Benn, S.I. (1982) 'Individuality, autonomy and community' in Eugene Kamenka (ed.) *Community as a Social Ideal*, Edward Arnold, London.

Bentham, Jeremy see Parekh, Bhikhu.

Beran, Harry (1972) 'Ought, Obligation and Duty' *Australasian Journal of Philosophy*, 50, pp. 20-21.

—— (1976) 'Political Obligation and Democracy', *Australasian Journal of Philosophy*, 54, pp. 250-4.

—— (1977) 'In Defense of the Consent Theory of Political Obligation and Authority', *Ethics*, 87, pp. 260-71.

—— (1983) 'What is the Basis of Political Authority?' *The Monist*, 66, pp. 487-99.

—— (1984) 'A Liberal Theory of Secession', *Political Studies*, XXXII, pp. 21-31.

Berki, R.N. (1975) *Socialism*, Dent, London.

Brandt, R.B. (1964) 'The Concepts of Obligation and Duty', *Mind*, 73, pp. 374-93.

Brown, Stuart, (1974) *Political Philosophy*, Open University Press, Milton Keynes.

Brownsey, P.F. (1978) 'Hume and the Social Contract', *Philosophical Quarterly*, 28, pp. 132-48.

Burke, Edmund see Hill, B.L.W.

Burnheim, John (1981) 'Statistical Democracy', *Radical Philosophy*, No. 27, Spring 1981.

Casinelli, C.W. (1961) *The Politics of Freedom: An Analysis of the Modern Democratic State*, University of Washington Press, Seattle.

Cohen, Carl (1971) *Democracy*, The Free Press, New York.

Dahl, R.A. (1970) *After the Revolution*, Yale University Press, New Haven and London.

Dahl, R.A. and Tufte, E.R. (1973) *Size and Democracy*, Stanford University Press, Stanford.

Bibliography

Downie, R.S. (1964) *Government Action and Morality*, Macmillan, London.

Dworkin, Gerald (1971) 'Paternalism' in *Morality and the Law*, edited by Richard A. Wassershtrom, Wadsworth, California.

Finnis, John (1984) *Natural Law and Natural Rights*, Clarendon Press, Oxford.

Flathman, R.E. (1972) *Political Obligation*, Atheneum, New York.

—— (1980) *The Practice of Political Authority*. University of Chicago Press, Chicago.

Friedman, Richard B. (1973) 'On the Concept of Authority in Political Philosophy' in *Concepts in Social and Political Philosophy*, edited by R.E. Flathman, Macmillan, New York.

Friedrich, Carl J. (1972) *Tradition and Authority*, Macmillan, London.

Fuller, Lon L. (1976) *The Morality of Law*, Yale University Press, New Haven.

Gaus, Gerald F. (1983) *The Modern Liberal Theory of Man*, Croom Helm, London.

Gauthier, David P. (1969) *The Logic of Leviathan*, Oxford University Press, Oxford.

Gauthier, David (1976-77) 'The Social Contract as Ideology', *Philosophy and Public Affairs*, 6, pp. 130–64.

Gewirth, Alan (1962) 'Political Justice' in *Social Justice*, edited by R.B. Brandt, Prentice-Hall, Englewood Cliffs, pp. 119–69.

Gough, J.W. (1967) *The Social Contract*, 2nd edn., Oxford University Press, Oxford.

Graham, Keith (1982) 'Democracy and the Autonomous Moral Agent' in *Contemporary Political Philosophy*, edited by Keith Graham, Cambridge University Press, Cambridge.

Grice, Russell (1967) *The Grounds of Moral Judgement*, Cambridge University Press, Cambridge.

Hancock, Claude L. (1963) *The United States Constitution in Perspective*, Allyn and Bancon, Boston.

Hart, H.L.A. (1955) 'Are There Any Natural Rights?', *Philosophical Review*, 64, pp. 175–97.

—— (1963) 'The Ascription of Responsibility and Rights', in *Logic and Language*, (first series) ed. by Antony Flew, Basil Blackwell, Oxford, pp. 145–66.

—— (1965) *The Concept of Law*, Oxford University Press, Oxford.

—— (1968) *Punishment and Responsibility*, Clarendon Press, Oxford.

—— (1969) *Law, Liberty and Morality*, Oxford University Press, Oxford.

Hickie, David (1985) *The Prince and the Premier*, Angus and Robertson, Sydney.

Hill, B.L.W. (ed.) (1975) *Edmund Burke on Government Politics and Society*, 'Reflections on the Revolution in France', Harvester Press, Brighton.

Hobbes, Thomas (1962) *Leviathan*, Collins, London.

Hoffman, Stanley (1981) *Duties Beyond Borders*, Syracuse University Press, Syracuse.

Hume, David see Aiken, Henry D.

Hunter, J.F.M. (1966) 'The Logic of Social Contracts', *Dialogue, Canadian Philosophical Review*, 5, pp. 31–46.

Johnson, Karen (1975) 'Political Obligation and the Voluntary Association Model of the State', *Ethics*, 86, pp. 17–29.

Kamanu, Onyeonoro S. (1974) 'Secession and the Right to Self-Determin-

Bibliography

ation: an O.A.U. Dilemma', *The Journal of Modern African Studies*, 12, pp. 355-76.
Lee, Desmond (trans.) (1975) Plato, *The Republic*, 2nd edn., Penguin Books, Harmondsworth.
Kant, Immanuel see Reiss, Hans.
Lewis, H.D. (1940) 'Is There a Social Contract?', *Philosophy*, 15, pp. 64-79 and 177-89.
Locke, John (1962) *Two Treatises of Civil Government*, Dent, London.
MacCormick, Neil (1979) 'Law, Obligation and Consent', *Archiv fuer Rechts- und Sozialphilosophie*, 65, pp. 387-411.
MacDonald, Margaret (1963) 'The Language of Political Theory' in *Logic and Language*, (first series) edited by Antony Flew, Basil Blackwell, Oxford, pp. 167-86.
McMillan, John; Evans, Gareth and Storey, Haddon (eds.), (1983) *Australia's Constitution: Time for Change?*, Allen and Unwin, Sydney.
MacPherson, Thomas (1967) *Political Obligation*, Routledge and Kegan Paul, London.
Mayo, Bernard (1958) *Ethics and the Moral Life*, Macmillan, London.
Minogue, Kenneth R. (1978) 'Social Contract and Social Breakdown' in *Democracy, Consensus and Social Contract*, edited by Pierre Birnbaum, Jack Lively and Geraint Parry, Sage, London.
Molnar, G. (1967) 'Defeasible Propositions', *Australasian Journal of Philosophy*, 45, pp. 185-97.
Monro, D.H. (1967) 'Bentham, Jeremy' in *The Encyclopedia of Philosophy*, edited by P. Edwards, Macmillan, New York, vol. 1, p. 285.
Mothersill, Mary (1967) 'Duty' in *The Encyclopedia of Philosophy*, edited by P. Edwards, Macmillan, New York, Vol. 2, pp. 442-4.
Murphy, Jeffrie G. (1971) 'The Vietnam War and the Right to Resistance' in *Civil Disobedience and Violence*, edited by Jeffrie G. Murphy, Wadsworth Publishing Company, California, pp. 64-72.
Nozick, Robert (1974) *Anarchy, State and Utopia*, Blackwell, Oxford.
Oakeshott, Michael (1975) 'On Human Conduct', Clarendon Press, Oxford.
Parekh, Bhikhu (ed.) (1973) *Bentham's Political Thought*, Croom Helm, London.
—— (1975) *The Concept of Socialism*, Holmes and Mejer, New York.
Pateman, Carole (1979) *The Problem of Political Obligation*, John Wiley, Chichester.
Peters, R.S. (and Benn, S.I.) (1969) *Social Principles and the Democratic State*, Allen and Unwin, London.
Peters, R.S. (1966) *Ethics and Education*, Allen and Unwin, London.
—— (1968) 'Authority' in *Political Philosophy*, edited by A. Quinton, Oxford University Press, Oxford, pp. 83-96.
Pitkin, Hanna (1965-6) 'Obligation and Consent I and II', *American Political Science Review*, 59-60, pp. 990-9 and 39-52. Reprinted in *Philosophy, Politics and Society*, Fourth Series, edited by P. Laslett, W.G. Runciman and Q. Skinner, Blackwell, Oxford, 1972.
Plamenatz, John (1967) *Man and Society*, Vol. 1, Longman, London.
Plato see Lee, Desmond.
Prichard, H.A. (1968) *Moral Obligation*, Oxford University Press, Oxford.
Pritchard, Michael S. (1973) 'Wolff's Anarchism', *The Journal of Value Inquiry*,

Bibliography

VII, pp. 296-302.

Quinton, Anthony (1968) (ed.) *Political Philosophy*, Oxford University Press, Oxford.

Raphael, D.D. (1970) *Problems of Political Philosophy*, Macmillan, London.

Rawls, John (1955) 'Two Concepts of Rules', *Philosophical Review*, 64 pp. 3-32.

—— (1964) 'Legal Obligation and the Duty of Fair Play' in *Law and Philosophy*, edited by Sydney Hook, University Press, New York, 1964, pp. 3-18.

—— (1971) *A Theory of Justice*, Harvard University Press, Cambridge.

Raz, Joseph (1975) *Practical Reason and Norms*, Hutchinson Unviersity Library, London.

—— (1979) *The Authority of Law*, Clarendon Press, Oxford.

Rees, J.C. (1954) 'The Limitations of Political Theory', *Political Studies*, 2, pp. 242-57.

Reiss, Hans (ed.) (1971) *Kant's Political Writings*, translated by H.B. Nisbet, Cambridge University Press, Cambridge.

Richards, David A.J. (1971) *A Theory of Reasons for Action*, Clarendon Press, Oxford.

Riley, Patrick (1982) *Will and Political Legitimacy*, Harvard University Press, Cambridge, Mass.

Ronen, Dov (1979) *The Quest for Self-Determination*, Yale University Press, New Haven and London.

Ross, W.D. (1930) *The Right and the Good*, Oxford University Press, Oxford.

Rousseau, Jean-Jacques see Cole, G.D.H.

Schick, F. (1980) 'Towards a Logic of Liberalism', *The Journal of Philosophy*, LXXVII, pp. 80-98.

Searle, John (1978) '*Prima Facie* Obligations' in *Practical Reasoning*, edited by Joseph Raz, Oxford University Press, pp. 81-90.

Simmons, A.J. (1979) *Moral Principles and Political Obligations*, Princeton University Press, Princeton.

Singer, Peter (1973) *Democracy and Disobedience*, Clarendon Press, Oxford.

Smith, Malcolm B.E. (1973) 'Wolff's Argument for Anarchism', *The Journal of Value Inquiry*, VII, pp. 290-95.

Steinberg, Jules (1978) *Locke, Rousseau, and the Idea of Consent*, Greenwood Press, Westport.

Tussman, Joseph (1960) *Obligation and the Body Politic*, Oxford University Press, New York.

von Wright, Georg Henrik (1964) *The Varieties of Goodness*, Routledge and Kegan Paul, London.

Walzer, Michael (1970) *Obligations: Essays on Disobedience, War and Citizenship*, Harvard University Press, Cambridge.

Warnock G.J. (1971) *The Object of Morality*, Methuen, London.

Watt, E.D. (1982) *Authority*, Croom Helm, London.

Weldon, T.D. (1953) *The Vocabulary of Politics*, Penguin Books, Harmondsworth.

Wight, Martin (1972) 'International Legitimacy', *International Studies*, Vol. 4, No. 1.

Wolff, Robert Paul (1969) 'On Violence, *The Journal of Philosophy*, pp. 601-16.

—— (1970) *In Defense of Anarchism*, Harper and Row, New York.

—— (1973) 'Reply to Professors Pritchard and Smith', *The Journal of Value Inquiry*, VII, pp. 303-6.

Bibliography

Woozley, A.D. (1979) *Law and Obedience: The Arguments of Plato's* Crito, Duckworth, London.

Further References

Abbott, Philip (1976) *The Shotgun Behind the Door*, University of Georgia Press, Athens, Ga.

Anscombe, Elizabeth (1978) 'On the Source of the Authority of the State', *Ratio*, pp. 1–28.

Bedau, H.A. (1969) *Civil Disobedience: Theory and Practice*, Pegasus, New York.

Braybrooke, David (1976) 'The Insoluble Problem of the Social Contract', *Dialogue: Canadian Philosophical Review*, XV, pp. 3–37.

Brennan, Tom (1981) *Political Education and Democracy*, Cambridge University Press, Cambridge.

Buchheit, Lee C. (1978) *Secession: The Legitimacy of Self-Determination*, Yale University Press, New Haven.

Cranston, Maurice (1967) *Freedom: A New Analysis*, 3rd edn., Longman, London.

Dunn, John (1980) *Political Obligation in its Historical Context*, Cambridge University Press, Cambridge.

Dworkin, Ronald (1978) 'Liberalism' in *Public and Private Morality*, edited by S. Hampshire, Cambridge University Press, Cambridge.

Hare, R.M. (1967) 'Lawful Government' in *Philosophy, Politics and Society*, Third series, edited by Peter Laslett and W.G. Runciman, Basil Blackwell, Oxford, pp. 157–72.

—— (1976) 'Political Obligation' in *Social Ends and Political Means*, edited by Ted Honderich, Routledge and Kegan Paul, London.

Hart, H.L.A. (1958) 'Legal and Moral Obligation' in *Essays in Moral Philosophy*, edited by A.I. Meldon, University of Washington Press, Seattle.

Kann, Mark E. (1978) 'The Dialectic of Consent Theory', *Journal of Politics*, 40, pp. 386–408.

Lee, R.W. (1898) *The Social Compact*, Oxford.

Lorber, Neil M. (1972) 'Social Rights, Majority Rule, and the Right of Secession', *Journal of Political Science* (New Zealand), 24, pp. 22–7.

Mackie, J.L. (1981) 'Obligations to obey the Law', *Virginia Law Review*, 67, pp. 143–58.

Manning, D.J. (1976) *Liberalism*, Dent, London.

Mish'alani, J.K. (1969) ' "Duty", "Obligation", and "Ought" ', *Analysis*, 30, pp. 33–40.

Murphy, Jeffrie G. (ed.) (1971) *Civil Disobedience and Violence*, Wadsworth, California.

Partridge, P.H. (1971) *Consent and Consensus*, Macmillan, London.

Pennock, J.R. and Chapman, J.W. (eds.) (1970) *Political and Legal Obligation*, Atherton Press, New York.

Plamenatz, J.P. (1968) *Consent, Freedom and Political Obligation* 2nd edn., Oxford University Press, Oxford.

Plamenatz, John (ed.) (1965) *Readings from the Liberal Writers*, Allen and Unwin, London.

160

Bibliography

Raz, Joseph (1981) 'Authority and Consent', *Virgina Law Review*, 67, pp. 103–31.

Sargent, Lyman Tower (ed.) (1979) *Consent: Concept, Capacity Conditions, and Constraints*, Franz Steiner, Wiesbaden.

Smith, M.B.E. (1973) 'Is There a *Prima Facie* Obligation to Obey the Law?', *Yale Law Journal*, 82.

Wasserstrom, Richard (1975) 'The Obligation to obey the Law', in *Today's Moral Problems*, edited by R. Wasserstrom, Macmillan Press, New York.

Wolff, Robert Paul (1968) *The Poverty of Liberalism*, Beacon Press, Boston.

Zinn, Howard (1968) *Disobedience and Democracy*, Random House, New York.

Author Index

Subject Index

For Product Safety Concerns and Information please contact our EU
representative GPSR@taylorandfrancis.com
Taylor & Francis Verlag GmbH, Kaufingerstraße 24, 80331 München, Germany

www.ingramcontent.com/pod-product-compliance
Lightning Source LLC
Chambersburg PA
CBHW050716280326
41926CB00088B/3044

9 780367 230890